"*Unstitched* is riveting, compassionate, topical, and one of the best books I've read this year. Stanciu, in beautiful prose, takes on the impact of the opioid epidemic on a small Vermont town with the gusto and suspense of a fine mystery novel, and the empathy that only a truly fine observer of the human condition could muster. Highly recommended."
— Thomas Christopher Greene, author of *The Perfect Liar*

"The shift in scale throughout *Unstitched* — from a tiny Vermont library, from one person's annoyance with one addict's break-ins, to the global scope of the opioid epidemic — is gut-wrenching. In a memoir that is generous and capacious at the same time that it is intimate, difficult, and finely wrought, readers will be carried by this deftly woven investigation into addiction in a small town. I didn't want to read this book, given my own family's loss, and then I couldn't put it down. *Unstitched* is the book about addiction that everyone needs to read — if we are ever to understand what needs to be done."
— Kerrin McCadden, author of *Keep This To Yourself*

"*Unstitched* should be mandatory reading. It is a heartbreaking, raw, tender and revelatory look at addiction and its pervasive grip on ourselves, our families, our communities, and our rural towns. This book undid me as I read — taking me into the heart of suffering, revealing my own habits, biases and fears — and then it gathered those pieces together and braided them into something new: a vision of hope, connection, possibility and healing for us all."
— Robin MacArthur, author of
Heart Spring Mountain and *Half Wild*

"While *Unstitched* begins as a true crime memoir set in an idyllic small Vermont town, soon it explodes into an exploration about 'the ugliness of poverty, the ravages of drug addiction' as Stanciu studies our nation's and her own addiction crises. Stanciu shines a light on the things we don't want to see: drug and alcohol abuse spread throughout our hometowns, including her own. Stanciu's beautiful light, and stunning writing, transforms those who are considered 'once a junkie, always a junkie,' into our friends and neighbors — where 'recovery is possible' and 'we are alike.'"

— Sean Prentiss, author of *Finding Abbey* and *Crosscut: Poems*

"With this thoughtful and thought-provoking book, Brett Stanciu shines a light on the twin tragedies of addiction and suicide that have infiltrated every family in America, even more so during the pandemic . . . Addiction, and all the dark aspects associated with it, is a subject I'd like to ignore. But ignoring it isn't going to help or make it go away, and Brett's book has led me to re-examine what I could do to be part of the solution. This book may provide a lifeline to someone in need, and might begin a conversation that saves a life."

— Natalie Kinsey-Warnock, author of *As Long As There Are Mountains* and *The Canada Geese Quilt*

"Beautifully crafted and researched, this book is for everyone, whether you've known the secret pain of addiction in your family or seen it ravaging your community. A luminous act of compassion and courage."

— Diana Whitney, author of *You Don't Have to Be Everything*

"With compassion, curiosity, and a fine eye for detail, Brett Ann Stanciu takes us on an unforgettable journey into the world of addiction and recovery in rural Vermont. The result is a beautiful and affecting story about the resilience of spirit and of community, at precisely the time we most need an abundance of both."

— Ben Hewitt, author of *The Town That Food Saved* and *Homegrown*

"I took a sobering read through this book because it focuses a lot on community, conversation, Vermont and the effects/impacts of substance abuse on all lives involved."

— Jason Broughton, Vermont state librarian and commissioner

unstitched

unstitched

MY JOURNEY TO UNDERSTAND OPIOID ADDICTION AND HOW PEOPLE AND COMMUNITIES CAN HEAL

BRETT ANN STANCIU

STEERFORTH PRESS
LEBANON, NEW HAMPSHIRE

For information about permission to reproduce
selections from this book, write to:
Steerforth Press L.L.C., 31 Hanover Street, Suite 1
Lebanon, New Hampshire 03766

Cataloging-in-Publication Data is available from the Library of Congress

Printed in the United States of America

ISBN 978-1-58642-269-1

1 3 5 7 9 10 8 6 4 2

For Molly and Gabriela, beloved daughters.

And, again, for my father.

The past is the present, isn't it? It's the future, too.
We all try to lie out of that but life won't let us.
       — Eugene O'Neill, *Long Day's Journey into Night*

A plague of sighing and grief! It blows a man up like
a bladder.
       — Shakespeare, *King Henry IV, Part One*

contents

BODY

one

Seeking Shelter

On a cold-throttled Thursday afternoon in January, shortly after the holidays, library trustee Susan Greene walked in on an intruder in the Woodbury Library. Minutes before, a neighbor had messaged Susan after spying a local man named John Baker* hurrying around the back of the library. Though the library was closed, the lights had blazed on briefly, and she guessed Baker had broken in again. When Susan rushed through the front door and saw Baker, she grabbed the desk phone and shouted that she was dialing 911. Baker fled through the side door. Then Susan called me, the librarian of this one-room rural Vermont library.

I was home folding laundry. That day, with a forecast high of fourteen degrees below zero, the superintendent had canceled school. At that temperature, buses couldn't run reliably, and some kids who lived in the village and walked to school lacked winter clothing. When I hung up the phone, I told my twelve-year-old daughter, Gabriela, who was rolling out biscuit dough, that I would be back as soon as I could.

She paused, her floury hands on the marble pin. "You okay?"

"I'll call. Your sister will be home soon."

Rushing out of the house, I forgot my gloves. As I drove the seven minutes from Hardwick, where I live, to Woodbury, I blew hard on one hand, then the other, to warm my fingers.

Over the past year, John Baker, a rumored heroin user, had repeatedly broken into the library. I hoped the camera I'd hidden in the library bookshelves had snapped a photo of him; the state's attorney had bungled a previous charge, and I needed evidence to reopen the case.

---

*Some names have been changed in this creative nonfiction work.

When I arrived at the library, Susan's husband, Randy, and their two teenagers were standing just inside the front door. Her willowy hips leaned against my desk. The fluorescent lights glared. With the heat turned down and the day so cold, clumps of snow tracked in by our boots hadn't melted into the hard-worn gray carpet.

"What happened?" I asked.

Each of them stared at different places — Randy at his wife; their daughter, Rachel, at a spider plant on the windowsill — but avoided my eyes. No one said anything.

I had known Susan for several years and knew she had a habit of pausing to stare right or left before she spoke, judicious with her words.

I repeated, "What happened?"

Randy answered, "The dispatcher on the neighbor's scanner said Baker shot himself. The ambulance is on its way."

"What? John Baker shot himself?"

Randy shifted his weight from one foot to the other. "That's what was called in."

"But he was just here?"

"He ran home and shot himself."

Less than half an hour had elapsed since Susan called me. I pulled my hat off my head and turned it around and around in my hands. My daughter had crocheted it from chunky turquoise yarn. "He shot himself over such a minor crime?"

Randy tugged on his insulated leather gloves. "Come on, kids. We're going home."

"Dad," his son, Ben, protested.

"I said, we're going home. Don't argue." He opened the door and held it while the teens walked out in the dark.

Shivering in the chilly room, I turned on the heater. Without removing my coat, I pulled up a chair on the public's side of my desk.

Susan hunched in my usual chair, facing the dark computer screen. "I doubt the state police will come here," she said. "They'll be too busy at his house. I'll walk down to the fire department later and ask what happened. You don't need to stay. I'll call you later."

On the desk between us, a facedown phone buzzed.

I unzipped my coat. "I'm staying." The phone vibrated again. "Do you want to answer that? Maybe it's your family."

"It's his. He dropped it in the snow when he ran out. I followed him — I was yelling — and found it."

The phone lay on my desk beside a bright orange origami box a boy had folded for me. Inside the box were secreted a large green paper clip, a plastic pig, and a purple yarn bracelet a child had made and forgotten. We waited in the quiet without speaking, the phone sporadically buzzing.

The heater whooshed on. I walked around and watered the plants. Pausing at the window, I cupped my hands around my eyes near the cold glass, peering into the darkness, and saw nothing but the reflection of my two eyes staring back at me.

Nearly two hours later, Rachel returned with news. The Bakers live on one side of Route 14, and the Greenes live on the other. "The ambulance left their house, and the chief's car is back at the station."

Susan stood up. "Did you hear? Is he alive?"

"I don't know. Let's go ask the chief."

We zipped up our coats. In the darkness, I fumbled sticking the key in the door lock. The exterior library light had blown out before Christmas, and I hadn't replaced it. We walked in silence to the fire department, a short distance down a slight hill. I cinched my scarf tighter around my face. Clouds screened the stars and the moon. At the fire department, we filed in the back door, where we found the chief, Paul Cerutti, sitting at a desk so large it dwarfed him, filling out paperwork.

He set down his pen. When not serving as the volunteer fire chief, Cerutti works as a fire safety inspector.

Susan asked, "Is he . . . ?"

"It's not your fault," Cerutti answered calmly.

"He's dead?"

"He's dead all right. Did it in the room where his parents keep firewood. My guys are cleaning up."

Susan shuddered. I was afraid she would fall over. Rachel and I wrapped our arms around her.

"Go home," Cerutti said. "The state police don't need anything from you. You've done nothing wrong. Listen, I've spent years trying to help people. The problem, mostly, is the people."

Susan stepped out of our arms and placed Baker's phone on the edge of the chief's desk. "It's his. I don't know what to do with it."

"I'll get it to where it needs to go." Cerutti leaned back in his chair and studied Susan. "Don't beat yourself up. If you need help getting over this, just ask. No shame there. Sometimes the hardest thing is to ask for help when you need it."

On the verge of crying, she crossed her arms over her chest and headed for the door. Following her and Rachel, I said over my shoulder, "Thank you."

Without standing, Cerutti opened his desk drawer, deposited Baker's phone inside, and slid the drawer shut. "I mean it about help. We've all been there."

Outside, we paused under the upside-down luminous cone of the door lamp. In our bulky jackets, the three of us embraced. Then Susan drew back and told her daughter, "Let's go home." They crossed Route 14 and disappeared into their clapboard house.

I walked back to my car, hands jammed in my coat pockets. I passed the unlit Episcopal church, my bootheels striking the icy road, the sole sound in the night. Above my scarf, the cold clawed at my eyes and forehead.

I drove home, my headlights splitting the darkness as I left the village and headed down the mountain pass. On this frigidly hostile night, the roads were empty. After I pulled into our driveway, I sat for a few moments. The cold crept into my lap and slunk beneath the collar of my coat. I imagined Susan standing outside the library, shouting, watching Baker run away, his phone falling from his pocket.

Wait, I thought. But it was too late.

⁇

That January, the bitter cold lingered. I imagined Baker's parents —
people I had never met — walking into their wood room every day,
gathering fuel to heat their home. Had they money, I wondered if
they would have left that house and town.

⁇

North to south, state highway Route 14 bisects Woodbury, a town
flanked by mountains on either side. Eons ago, the incremental
shifting of glaciers sheared off the prehistoric peaks that once
towered higher than the snowy Himalayas, rounding their jagged
tips to rocky humps. A wetland glimmers on the village outskirts; in
the summer, the glassy water sparkles with a covering of velvety
pearl-and-gold water lilies. Along the edges, beavers build and
rebuild their dams, and muskrats lay claim to this marshy space with
their stick homes. Moose, herons, songbirds, and insects thrive here.

Just beyond the wetland, the town raised a two-story red schoolhouse shortly after the beginning of World War I. Today the
Woodbury School, its student population diminished over the years,
has fewer than fifty students from kindergarten to grade six. Perched
on a hill and surrounded by forest, the school overlooks a playground, vegetable gardens, and a ball field. A right-hand turn from
the school's gravel parking lot leads to Route 14. The pavement
switchbacks down a shadowy mountain pass to Hardwick, where
I've lived for three years since selling our Woodbury house. Turn left
from the school instead, and the dirt roads meander for miles among
woods and ponds.

My younger daughter graduated from the Woodbury School in a
sixth-grade class of three girls and three boys. In her class, one family
vacationed in Portugal and Aruba. Another frequented the local
food shelf. Gabriela knew who wore the nicest clothes, who had a
passion for dirt bikes, and who had a fine singing voice and wanted

to study music. She also understood how each classmate's family reputation fit into town — whose mother ran a popular daycare and whose older brothers got into trouble at high school.

Like many others, I arrived here as a transplant. As a child and into my twenties, I moved frequently, from deserty New Mexico to New Hampshire's red-brick mill cities to mountainous western Washington. Gradually, I became smitten with this tight-knit town. I joined the five-member school board and chaperoned walks into the wetlands. Our world was stitched together by carving jack-o'-lanterns, giggling at sleepovers, voting yay or nay on town and school budgets at community meetings, and baking surprise birthday cakes for friends. When I discovered that the library had been broken into after hours, what remained was a lingering residue not only of cigarette smoke but also of fear. I began to wonder if maybe this world wasn't so fine.

◌∞◌

The first time I suspected that an intruder had entered the library, I was bewildered.

I discovered the break-in on a sunny Monday in early September. I had recently taken the job as librarian to supplement my income from writing for a parenting magazine. That morning, when I unlocked the library door, I walked into cigarette smoke so dense that I coughed and propped open the door to air out the room. I checked my desk and discovered the cash bag and its twenty-dollar bill were missing. Stepping outside to escape the smoke, I phoned Susan. "I know this seems bizarre, but I think someone broke into the library over the weekend. The petty cash is gone, and the space reeks like someone was smoking cigarettes for a prolonged period."

"Call the police. We've had this problem before. You know John Baker? Lives in the village with his folks?"

"I don't think so."

"A few years ago, before you were hired, the school board chair caught him one night in the library. The school's lawyer had a 'no trespass' order served, so he isn't supposed to be on the grounds. He must be at it again."

"Why didn't I know this?" I paced in a tight circle on the grass.

"I thought everyone knew. I mean, we figured he'd been breaking in for years, before he got caught. Anyway, give the state police a call. If they're not too busy, they might come out. Either way, we'll need a record of this."

As a small rural town, Woodbury has no local law enforcement. When Susan hung up, I dialed the state police barracks, a forty-minute drive away in Middlesex. When the dispatcher answered on the third ring, I said, "I'm Brett Stanciu, the librarian in Woodbury. It's not an emergency, but our town library has been burglarized." I explained about the smoke and the missing money.

"There's no immediate danger, is there? No property damage, no evidence, no reason for a trooper to drive all the way out to Woodbury?"

"Well, what am I supposed to do?"

"We're going to need more than your suspicions. Maintenance could have been smoking a cigarette. Maybe the money was misplaced?"

"Really?"

"I'm sorry, ma'am, but I'll need something more. Some kind of solid evidence."

I hung up the phone with a bang. Solid evidence or not, I knew someone had been in the library that weekend.

∾

As the September days slowly cooled, cigarette smoke greeted me randomly every two weeks or so when I unlocked the library door, but I didn't call the state police again. Why cause a fuss when the police wouldn't come out, anyway? Recently divorced and unable to collect child support, I relied on the income from my librarian salary to pay my bills; I was working hard to succeed at this new job. I replaced the missing money with a twenty from my own wallet and started keeping the petty cash hidden in a DVD about the history of Jesus.

One day, a patron handed me a dollar to pay for an overdue library book. Distracted, I set the dollar inside my top desk drawer, under a pair of scissors. When I looked for the money a few days later, the bill was gone.

Really? I thought. Who would take a dollar from a public library? But I said nothing. It was just a dollar, and maybe I had misplaced it.

At trustee meetings that fall, between discussing the budget and upcoming poetry readings, we gossiped about Baker. In his early thirties, he still lived at home. Rumors circulated that he had overdosed in a car in Hardwick's Tops Supermarket parking lot, and the rescue squad had revived him with Narcan.* During the library's afterschool program, a parent confided to me that he had seen Baker one weekend walking behind the library with a six-pack of beer clutched under his arm. He drove with no registration or driver's license and worked for a construction crew that allegedly hired drug users. Baker, the parent told me, was a problem I didn't need.

The next Saturday, Chrissy Skelton, a churchgoing stay-at-home mother with twin kindergartners, stopped in before noon. As she approached me, her girls disappeared behind the tall wooden dollhouse, murmuring a make-believe story about plastic piglets who slept in the bathtub.

Wearing a calico A-line skirt well below her knees, Chrissy stood beside my desk and said quietly, "I hear you're having troubles with a certain person again." She winked her right eye once, as if we shared a confidence.

I glanced up from reading email. "Maybe. Or maybe it's nothing."

She leaned over my laptop. "I've lived in this town for years."

"What are you saying?"

---

*A nasal spray, Narcan is the brand name of naloxone — an opioid antagonist designed to rapidly reverse an opioid overdose. Since 2014, the Vermont Health Department has offered free Narcan at designated sites.

"Once a junkie, always a junkie. Be careful, is all." Chrissy smiled conspiratorially.

"I am, of course. I mean, I called the police." Before I could ask if she had more information, a woman who had requested the newest Louise Penny book walked in.

The truth is, I was afraid. What if I found Baker unconscious after an overdose?

Another month passed. Some days, cigarette smoke met me at the door; other days, the library smelled of its usual elementary school scent of crayons. The inconsistency was unnerving. Finally, Susan borrowed a small game camera, triggered by motion to snap photos. At the end of every day, before I went home, I hid the camera in the bookshelves. Within a week, I had photos. The images showed Baker sitting at my desk, the worn wood surface cluttered with picture books and a flock of misshapen colored clay chickens made by a boy named Trevor, a note written in Magic Marker to Miss Brett taped to the computer monitor.

Until I saw the hazy, black-and-white photos of this frowning stranger sitting in my chair, I hadn't entirely believed he had been in the library. But he was.

This time, a trooper drove to Woodbury when I called. He took copies of the photos but warned me that the legal system would likely be lenient.

"What does that mean?"

"He'll probably get off. Just letting you know."

Later that week, Susan stopped in. "I got gossip at the post office."

"Hold on." I held up my hand, saved where I was in a grant application for children's books, and then closed my laptop. "Let's hear it."

"After the trooper came out that morning, he drove over to Baker's parents' house and arrested him. He's out of the lockup now, of course, but he's moved out of his parents' place, and he's sleeping in his truck in the post office parking lot. With a court date coming up, I doubt he'll be back here. Good thing, as I have to return that game camera. Hunting season's coming up."

∽

As the foliage transformed from green to pale gold to flaming red, the state's attorney's office sent occasional letters or emails about the case. I submitted a statement. Then one day I received an email notifying me that the charges against Baker had been dropped, with no explanation.

On that exceptionally warm afternoon, I took the phone outside with me and called the state's attorney, Scott Williams. Scott had roomed down the hall from me in our freshman dorm at Marlboro College near Brattleboro, Vermont. When he picked up, Scott asked, "You mind talking to me while I walk out? I'm late to pick up my daughter."

"Okay, fine. In brief, I'm calling about charges you dropped against John Baker, who broke into the Woodbury Library. I'd like to know why nothing's happening. I had photos for evidence and everything."

"I'd have to look at the case again to get the details. What's the story with this guy? I don't want to saddle him with something serious if it's not a big deal."

"I'm not trying to get revenge. But he's been breaking in for months now. And he was doing the same thing before my time. It's a public library, Scott, on school grounds."

I heard him breathe heavily as he walked.

"Look, Scott, I'm asking for something serious enough to keep him out. There's a playground around the library. What if someone sees him tumbling in through the window? You get my drift? What if something bigger happens?"

"Okay. Got it. Look, do me a favor." I heard a beep as he unlocked his car. "Send me an email reminding me what we discussed, and I'll reopen his case tomorrow."

"Thank you. I appreciate it. We'll talk soon."

I sent the email, but I never heard back. Instead, a few days later I read in the paper that Scott had unexpectedly taken personal leave. I called the state's attorney's office but couldn't get past the receptionist.

The case was never reopened. Nonetheless, I hoped the charges — even though they were dismissed — would be enough to deter Baker from returning to the library.

For a few weeks, I believed this was possible. As the days shortened and the November gray descended, the library remained free of cigarette smoke. A single mother working two jobs, my life churned along — keeping my checkbook in the black, meals on the table, homework done, the laundry perpetually cycling. In my garden, the sunflowers' green and gold ebbed to brown. Birds raided seeds from the flowers' heavy faces. Autumn dulled to bleak December.

Then, early one morning shortly before Christmas, I was reading email on the couch and drinking coffee. The school's grounds and maintenance man wrote that he had seen footprints in the snow around the library. "Our friend appears to be back." I closed my laptop. I was beginning to wonder if I was a minor character in a much larger story, where the plotline wasn't clear to me.

That morning, when I unlocked the library door, the room reeked of cigarettes. Without taking off my coat, I stood at my desk and phoned the state police. After a few minutes, the trooper who had arrested Baker that fall came on the line.

"Did that camera get any more photos?" the trooper asked.

"I removed it. Why would I need more evidence?" With my blue pen, I wrote "evidence" on a sticky note, drew a rectangle around it, and then surrounded it with question marks. "Then the state's attorney dropped the charges. I don't know why. I never got an answer back from the office, although I called and called."

Over the line, I heard the trooper sigh. "I can't do anything about what the state's attorney's office does."

"You need another photo?"

"That would be helpful."

"Fine. We can start this all over again." I thanked him for his time, hung up, and groaned.

The art teacher had wandered in during a break between her classes and was browsing the shelf of new adult fiction. She lifted one eyebrow. "Trouble? I'm sensing some frustration."

"Some? Try a tidal wave. The library has an intruder again."

"Again? What are you going to do?"

"Honestly, I don't know. What are my options, anyway? Am I supposed to nail the windows shut?" I stood and lifted up the coffee-pot. "Want some? I'm about to make a pot for the afternoon."

"That sounds wonderful. I'll get the fifth and sixth graders set up and come back." She disappeared into her room next door.

While the coffee dripped, I pulled out the manila folder I'd labeled "Break-In" and picked up the phone. Months ago, the victim's advocate at the state's attorney's office had called me about the impact statement, and I wondered if she could help me now. Luckily, she was in her office when I dialed and picked up. "Why do I need to get another photo?" I asked. "The state police already have evidence. Why can't they just reopen the case?"

"I understand your frustration."

"Do you really? I know this guy has been breaking in. The rumor around town is that he's using drugs. Still, the state police won't come out. One of my trustees is so mad she's planning to sleep here at night until she catches him. What if one day I walk in and find him dead from an overdose? This situation is totally out of hand."

"I'll see if I can talk to the interim state's attorney. I'll run down the hall now, as I think she's here today. Hopefully, I can get the case opened. I'll call you back, okay?"

But she didn't call back — not that day, or the next. She never returned my call, and the case stayed closed.

∽

My days were crammed with learning to host class visits and filling requests for mysteries and biographies. When hunting season ended, I borrowed the camera again and hid it in the row of adult biographies. Weeks passed and the camera caught nothing. Still, I had a perpetual sense of unease. When would I unlock the door and walk into cigarette smoke again?

My daughters and I shared a Christmas dinner of roasted turkey with friends. After my divorce, I anticipated the end of the holidays, that sweet spot where presents of puzzles and art supplies had satisfied everyone. There with friends I could breathe, relieved that we had surmounted another holiday. In that season, everyone else's family but ours seemed intact, much as I knew that was ridiculous.

Then shortly after the new year, on that frigid afternoon, Susan phoned me from the library.

I have what I believe are the final photos of John Baker. In one, he's walking across the room to turn off the motion-activated lights that must have flashed on when he tumbled through the window. The next photos are fuzzy; the lights are off. In these, Baker is standing behind my desk. What he's doing I can't determine. The final image captured by that camera shows Susan leaning against the desk, talking on the phone — to me or the state police — her face haggard.

✑

The night John Baker died, snow dusted around our house. The next morning, Friday, school was canceled again due to the frigid cold snap. When I left the house, my daughters were still sleeping.

As I unlocked the library door, the phone was ringing.

"Yes?" I answered. "Woodbury Library."

"It's Chrissy. You heard?" she snickered. "I read the news in the paper this morning. Sounds like that Baker character won't be bothering you anymore."

"So I understand."

"I didn't mean — you know, I didn't mean . . ."

"I know."

"Actually, I called for a friend, not about that. The McConnells, who moved in down the road from me? They have a baby boy, and I heard you're having a family library social tomorrow morning, right? I wanted to let them know the time."

"Ten thirty."

"That's so great that you're getting these families together. I'd come with the twins, but it's Bob's mother's birthday brunch."

I stared out the window at the trail of my boot prints in the snow.

"His mother will be seventy-three. Just to break up the winter blahs, we decided to do a tapas brunch. I'm baking these phyllo spinach and feta spirals . . ." Then she said, "He was just a junkie, you know."

A few snowflakes the size of nickels spun earthward. The forecast predicted snow all day. "So I understand." I hung up the phone.

Without turning on the lights, I stood in the dark, quiet library, studying the table where Baker had been sitting when Susan walked in. On its back corner sat a white china teacup, factory-painted with a faded pink rose, a thorny vine, and two unopened buds. The cup was part of a set of five that were usually stored upside down beneath the microwave in the adjacent art room. The children used them to hold beads and sequins. Pieces of a now broken-apart set, these cups held a hidden history, a reminder that this library and this town had countless stories I didn't know — and never would.

I walked over to the table, lifted the cup, half full of water, and turned it around and around in my hands. The last time I had seen John Baker was a sunny October afternoon. I was walking from the post office to the library, my arms wrapped around packaged books and envelopes, taking my time in the autumn warmth and admiring the sugar maples glowing scarlet and gold. Baker, wearing a plaid shirt and work boots and in need of a shave, sat on the front granite steps of the Episcopal church. The church holds sporadic services for a handful of elderly parishioners during the summer months and closes in the winter to save on heating costs. I lingered across the dirt road, watching Baker poke at his phone. A single crow flew over-

head. We were the only people in our tiny village square that afternoon. Within months, he would be dead.

What if, instead of passing him in silence, I had ignored all the
gossip and sat down beside him on that sun-warm granite step?

But I didn't. I walked up the dusty road and carried on with my
life.

At the end of that day after Baker's death, I took the cup home
with me and set it on my desk. Inside the cup, I noticed scratches
from rough washing and a residue of something I couldn't determine. I seemed to have been emptied out, too, and what remained
were traces of things I couldn't recognize.

two

Muddy Print

Saturday morning, the temperature dropped to nineteen degrees below zero, and my car cranked over reluctantly when I tried to start it. I turned the defroster on high to thaw the icy windshield, then stood inside at our living room window and contemplated exhaust puff from my silver Toyota's tailpipe, the pale poisonous clouds drifting apart and dissipating.

Our two-story, hundred-year-old house overlooks a small valley where streams and creeks feed into the Lamoille River. That dusky winter morning, scattered house lights twinkled. Smoke rose in white furls from chimneys, and a ghostly scrim of fog hovered over the frozen river. At the far end of the valley, the shifting mist parted and revealed an icy triangle of reservoir. The prior spring, as I walked along the reservoir's bank with my two daughters, two bald eagles swooped from an immense white pine so close that we heard the flap of their wings. The pair darted near the water, then rose and flew toward the sun, disappearing from our sight.

⁓

Cupped in a wooded valley along the Lamoille River, Hardwick village lies at the western edge of Vermont's Northeast Kingdom, so named for the three northeastern counties' pristine beauty. The fathomless lakes and abundant forests in this corner of the state harbor a population struggling to make do, mixed with "mailbox farmers" — those who receive a livelihood via trust fund checks and often drive battered Subarus. According to the most recent census, the Hardwick village population numbers approximately thirteen hundred. The whole township claims less than three thousand residents.

In the first half of the twentieth century, when Vermont claimed less than a hundred miles of paved roads, dairy farming reigned. Family farmers delivered raw milk in ten-gallon stainless steel cans to local creameries, where folks chewed the fat with neighbors while their cans were emptied. Beginning in the 1950s, the state mandated that bulk holding tanks replace those milk cans. Trucks collected milk at the barns, often bypassing the most remote homesteads; the steepest hillside farms yielded too little milk to merit a rugged trip, especially in winter. As small farms folded, forests gradually reclaimed fields across the landscape.

Hardwick's history was also shaped by stone. Just beyond the village center, Atkins Field — a rectangular green with an impressive post-and-beam gazebo and a row of spindly maple saplings — marks the site of the once-bustling granite hub. The dandelion-strewn grass skims over an infertile rubble, the debris of granite cutting sheds worked hard and dirty for decades until the industry slumped in World War I. Today a single sway-roofed, windowless cutting shed remains, dominating one side of the green. Nearly everything else from that era — save a handful of foundations that peek through the flourishing burdock and raspberry brambles, and the chunks of granite scattered through the nearby woods — has been burned or carted away.

Behind the listing shed lies a dirt mountain bike track for kids and the town's community garden, replete with raised beds, a green-house, blueberry bushes, and apple saplings. Through the golden-rod, a footpath meanders to the railroad bed, shadowed by forested Buffalo Mountain. In the years when the railroad ran in the moun-tain's shadow, steam-powered engines strewed cinders. During World War II, the tracks were torn up, sold for scrap metal, and converted to the war effort. The railbed is now a trail winding through wetlands and scrubby conifer stands, the past vanishing beneath vigorous saplings, vines, and wildflowers. Between the field and the mountain, a sturdy wooden bridge constructed for snow-mobiles crosses Cooper Brook. In spring or after storms, the stream floods and roars, and the pungent scents of wet soil and decaying leaves mingle.

Routes 14 and 15 curve through the village along the banks of the Lamoille River, briefly overlapping before 14 jags north to Craftsbury, while 15 and the river head west toward Lake Champlain. The Lamoille nourishes dairy, vegetable, and hemp farming and carries away the town's cleaned-up wastewater, too. In the summer, kayakers and anglers explore the water, while tourists snap photos of the famous wooden Fisher Covered Railroad Bridge, the last of its kind used for trains in the state. Fifty miles away, at prodigious Lake Champlain, the conjoined waters flow to the Richelieu River, then north to the Atlantic Ocean.

So much water. So many rivers, streams, and backyard trickles. So much ice.

∽

Shortly before eight that Saturday morning, I arrived at the library. I dropped an armload of interlibrary loan books on my desk, turned up the thermostat, and glanced at the library email inbox. I was expecting families shortly for the first of what I hoped would become a series of socials. In the deep cold, however, I wasn't sure how many of them would attend.

I looked around the room, searching for any small objects, like stray beads from craft projects, that a toddler might glean and mouth. The children's area, filled with baskets of toys and a wooden dollhouse, claims the library's sunniest corner. Adult stacks and a long table used for meetings dominate the room's center. Along the back wall is a station with two public-use computers and a smaller table often strewn with kids' paintings or felt scraps hand-stitched into doll's pillows.

On the rug in the children's space, I picked up a red plastic octopus and set it on a bookshelf. While crouching down to gather loose strands of orange embroidery thread, I paused. What if John Baker left something behind, like a needle or a crumpled cellophane bag? On my hands and knees, I peered behind the wall heater, under the computer table, and around the feet of my desk. I discovered only a child's green train engine beneath an armchair. On my feet again, I dropped the toy in the basket of wooden track pieces and train cars, where it landed with a clunk, startling me. I grabbed the high back of the upholstered wing chair and stared out the window at the gray sky, steadying myself.

After a moment, I unlocked the door, then straightened the messy graphic novels. A little after ten, Colin Mackin walked in, blinking as his glasses fogged up in the library's warm air. He was carrying his two-year-old daughter, Poppy, bundled in a pink snowsuit.

"Good morning," I called. "Coffee will be ready soon."

"Fantastic." Colin's bushy hair sprang wildly in all directions, as if it hadn't been combed in days. "We're teething. Joy is sick, so I took the night shift. Looks like I'm on for the day, too."

During the next half hour, the families filed in, lining up their snowy boots beside the door and piling coats on an armchair. The parents lounged on the rug or perched on child-sized chairs, cradling their babies in hand-knit sweaters and miniature hair bows and chatting about deals on diapers and how much sleep everyone was getting — or not.

A woman I didn't recognize whooshed in with her toddler, who was struggling to walk in his fat-soled winter boots. "I heard families were getting together today?"

I introduced myself, waved her toward the circle of parents, and offered a hot drink.

"Tea would be great," she said as she tugged a red coat off her child.

For the next two hours, the parents meandered around the library, talking and eating homemade anise cake a father had brought, abandoning half-drunk cups of milky coffee on my desk and the windowsills. I overheard one mother laugh as she shared her home-birth story: "I was on my hands and knees, howling. I didn't even remember the Mozart playlist I put so much effort into putting together! Sounds came out of me as she was born that I never imagined." As she spoke, her husband draped his arm around her shoulders, and her ruby-lipped babe slept tucked against her chest.

Two women old enough to be grandmothers stopped by to return books and stayed to hold babies. One girl, snuggled in her mother's lap, smiled at me as I passed by, gathering empty cups. When her mother heard me laugh, she turned and asked, "Did she smile at you? She's just discovered how to do it."

"What a little darling."

The mother resumed her conversation with a friend about the yellow her husband had painted their kitchen — "the color of melted butter." Another group of parents discussed the idea of building a trail network through the woods, connecting each of their houses, so the kids could one day walk or mountain bike without parents from home to home.

I refilled my coffee cup and leaned a hip against my desk, gazing out the window at the overcast sky spitting snowflakes. Half listening to the chatter, I wrapped my hands around the warm mug and wondered what these families were doing that late afternoon two days earlier when I received Susan's phone call — changing diapers, maybe, or cooking dinner. No one had mentioned anything about what had happened to John Baker; news of his death apparently hadn't reached them yet, if it ever would.

I gazed at a few toddlers pushing tiny trains around the rug and imagined how the lives of these families would unfold. Five or six years from now, these parents would attend school concerts and art shows together, maybe join the PTO or school board. They would adore or despise teachers, endlessly hashing over who assigned too much homework and who picked favorite students; they would swap babysitting duties, deliver homemade soup or chili to the sick, celebrate one another in times of joy — new babies, birthdays, holidays — and comfort one another through the loss of a grandparent or job. A few of these couples would divorce. I already wondered about one pair I noticed sniping at each other; beneath the jesting lay a sharp edge to their words. Another couple, sitting cross-legged on the carpet, held hands almost the whole time. I envisioned a raucous shindig for their fiftieth wedding anniversary.

But how would the future unroll for the young families in town who weren't here this morning, the ones who didn't follow the library's Facebook page or get invited by a friend, who didn't have a library card, or maybe just didn't care? In these towns, grocery shopping reveals a cultural and economic divide; people patronize either a chain supermarket or Hardwick's hippieish Buffalo Mountain Food Co-op, stocked with pricier organic produce and homemade beeswax candles. The groups have little crossover. The crowd that morning was mostly, but not entirely, co-op shoppers.

In one corner, a toddler who had been playing with wooden blocks dropped a cube on his toe and wailed. His mother scooped him into her arms and announced, "Naptime!" As if cued, the parents set down their coffee cups, restuffed their diaper bags, zipped their babies into snowsuits, thanked me, and headed home for lunch.

I vacuumed, washed the mugs, and rinsed out the coffeepot. The below-zero temperatures hadn't abated, and the forecast was for more snow, so I didn't expect many patrons that afternoon. I turned on a Vermont Public Radio podcast about recommended books soon to be released in 2018 and began uploading the photos I had snapped that morning to the library's Facebook page. Almost immediately, the Likes appeared.

∽

Monday morning after Baker's death, Amy Massé, the school principal, stopped into the library. I had served on the school board with her, and through countless hours of budget and visioning meetings we became friends. Over the weekend, I had sent her and the superintendent a short email explaining that Baker had been discovered in the library by a trustee and died shortly afterward at home of a self-inflicted gunshot wound.

"When I read your email," she said, "I just couldn't believe it." Amy walked around my desk and gave me a hug.

"I can't comprehend it, either. I'm beyond sorry. I keep thinking — what was I supposed to do? Pretend he wasn't hanging out at the library after hours?"

"You couldn't have done that. You're the librarian. And there's no way you could have seen this coming. You must know that."

"Maybe I could have done something differently?"

"No." About my height, Amy looked directly into my eyes, something few people do, as I am four foot nine.

"Brett, you never could have predicted this. Whatever was going on with him was much, much bigger than you."

I took some comfort from Amy's words. Driving home that afternoon, I repeated to myself that there was nothing I could have done.

∽

A few days later, another friend stopped by when no one else was in the library. "That man who died?" she asked quietly. "Was he the library intruder?"

I nodded.

"Ohhhh," she said.

But no one else said anything more to me. Although I had heard plenty about him when he was alive, when Baker died so did the rumors about him. The silence resounded.

I didn't know the family, and certainly didn't feel that I could send a sympathy card: too little, too late. What could I have possibly written?

∽

The following Saturday, Baker's memorial service was held. The cold snap continued. During recess, the children were kept inside. By three, when the after-school program began, the kids roamed the library aimlessly, eager to run wild. The adults sprawled in the library armchairs, exhausted. Spring seemed impossibly far away.

This story could have ended here; case closed. But while driving home or staring out the library window, my thoughts kept drifting to those final images of Baker sitting at my desk. How were a series of library break-ins connected to a man's death? What had I missed? I had focused on the physical facts — a missing window screen, a stolen dollar bill — and ignored the tangled story that bound these pieces together. I began to see, too, evidence of what I ignored in Vermont when it didn't directly touch me — the prison of class, the ugliness of poverty, the ravages of drug addiction. A failing court system, strapped law enforcement. Surely, these things were not unknown to the man who had died beside his parents' dwindling woodpile.

∽

A few weeks later, near the end of January, Chrissy Skelton and her children stopped by the library. Her husband was hammering down a wood floor in their basement, so she had taken the children sledding on the playground to get them out of the house. She draped their wet snow pants and jackets over a chair beside the heater to dry while the twins snacked on carrot sticks and dry Cheerios at the table.

After we chitchatted for a bit about the incrementally warming weather and the slick sledding, Chrissy lowered her voice and told me about a couple who was divorcing. "You wouldn't have guessed they'd split up. They seemed like such nice people. It just goes to show, you never know what happens behind closed doors. But — hey! — sometimes you need to get divorced. Fact of life. No judgment there."

I knelt and tidied the babies' board books on a bottom shelf.

Standing above me, she asked in a cheery voice, "So did you have to change your name after your divorce? How did that work out?

Because you and your ex-husband have different names now, right? Then again, you seem like the kind of person who might have kept yours from the get-go."

"I did."

"That was convenient. A blessing you probably never anticipated."

I walked across the room to the cluttered art table. Before Christmas, a patron had donated a box of small paint pots. I unscrewed the lids one by one and tossed the dried-up pots in the garbage pail.

In her white socks, Chrissy padded behind me. "Where is your ex-husband now?"

I threw the remaining paints in the garbage bin without opening the lids. "I have no idea."

She winked and said piously, "Pray he's safe."

My hand shook as I lifted a child's scissors, round-tipped with an orange plastic handle.

Chrissy added something I couldn't hear over the blood seething in my ears.

"Pray he's safe?" I repeated. "Pray he's safe?" My eyes brimmed with tears.

"What did I say? Why are you crying?"

I dropped the scissors on the table and met her eyes. "What do you know about me, anyway? My life is none of your business."

Crying now, too, Chrissy grabbed her family's wet clothes and Tupperware containers of Cheerios and carrots and hustled her children out the door.

When she left, I pulled the trash bag from the bin, knotted it, and stalked outside to the Dumpster. After I hurled the bag in, I stood on the sidewalk, shivering in my Danskos and blue dress. Wide flakes of snow swirled around me. With my fists, I wiped tears from my face and walked back into the library. "Pull it together," I whispered to myself. "Don't let Chrissy get under your skin." Soon I could lock up and head home to my daughters. Gabriela would be waiting, hungry, ready to make dinner with me. I had promised to bake chicken wings, one of her favorite meals. My oldest, Molly, a college student who lived with us, would be getting off her shift as an aide at a nearby nursing home.

Before leaving, I wiped down the sunflower-patterned plastic cloth draped over the art table and organized the mason jars of paintbrushes and colored pencils. In one corner, I straightened the cardboard boxes of used books donated for an upcoming book sale. Earlier that week, a patron had dug through the fantasy fiction and left me a mess. Suddenly, I had a desperate need for fresh air. I opened the window behind the boxes, braced my hands on the sill, and leaned my head and upper body out into the sharp cold. The plastic lid dangled cockeyed from the school's compost bin; frozen banana peels, apple cores, and withered purple cabbage were scattered in the fresh snow. I breathed in deeply, exhaled, then closed the window and locked it.

Stepping back, I noticed a smudge of mud on the wall beneath the window, about the size of the palm of my hand. In snow-covered January, the ground hadn't been bare in months. Looking closer, I saw that the screen was missing, and the window clasp had been scraped. Baker must have jimmied this window open with a pocketknife and climbed in. With a fingertip, I flicked away the crumbling soil.

The faintest smear remained.

I sat on the floor and leaned my back against the bookshelves. I stayed there so long that the lights switched off. At some point I thought about calling Gabriela to assure her that I'd be home soon. I thought of my younger daughter, her face still a pale nut brown from last summer's tan, cozied on the couch with her cats, watching through the living room window for my silver car to pull into the driveway. She might be worried or upset, but I knew she would run to the kitchen door to greet me happily when I arrived. The library closed at five, and that time had long passed. Dusk swept through the windows, darkening the shadows beneath the tables. At this twilight hour not so long ago, I would have been pouring myself a glass of wine. Summer or winter, that first sweet drink always seduced me with its warmth. For a few minutes, I could believe the illusion that all was well in the world.

The library was so dark I could no longer see the smear of mud on the wall. I grimaced, thinking of Chrissy's casual judgment the morning after Baker's death: "Once a junkie, always a junkie." But was my attitude any more kind? I had spent hours trying to get him arrested. I walked by without speaking when I saw him on the church steps. Why had I never asked what he wanted in the library? Was he seeking refuge from the cold? Or was there something else in this quiet space that he wanted? Why had I never extended an offer to come in through the door and not the window?

My cell phone rang. Leaping up, I hurried to my desk to answer. The fluorescent lights flashed on, stinging my eyes.

The caller was Gabriela. "Are you coming home?"

"I had a patron who lingered. I'm leaving now." With the phone pressed against my ear, I slid my laptop into my backpack, straightened the pens and picture books on my desk, and returned the scissors to the art table.

"Should I start dinner?"

"I'll be home in six minutes — really. I'm on my way out. Love you." I zipped up my coat, slid my backpack over my shoulder, and, my hand on the doorknob, stood gazing at that window where the screen was missing. The glass reflected my furrowed brow. I reached over and turned off the overhead lights, overriding the automatic shutoff. Enough daylight lingered that I saw my eyes, stripped of their woodsy brown, glistening with a residue of tears. So much winter remained. I wanted nothing to do with any of this.

three

Kindergarten Dreams

In early April, purple and blue crocuses emerged from the sun-warmed strip of soil rimming the schoolhouse — tiny gems of spring. Honking cacophonously, geese flew northward in broad, wavering Vs that stretched across the sky, like giant sewing needles stitching together the thawing lakes with the cloud-scattered sky. As winter melted, the Vermont Department of Libraries initiated a program offering free Narcan to libraries across the state. Via email, staff were requested to sign up for a two-hour session of a few presentations and instructions on how to use the nasal spray.

Our listserv crackled with discussion. One librarian wrote that her trustees, worried about liability, forbid her from attending. Two others countered that Narcan was free in Vermont, and anyone could legally administer it to someone who had overdosed. A staff member from one of the larger city libraries chimed in that, with people overdosing in Price Chopper bathrooms, she believed keeping Narcan in her library was a civic duty. Who wanted their library to be known as a place where someone died of a heroin overdose?

I had mixed feelings about attending. After Baker died, I had emailed the Department of Libraries what details I knew. By then, I had participated in numerous workshops at the DOL. I liked their staff and wanted their sympathy, which they gave me generously. I felt obligated to attend this training; clearly, opioids were available in Woodbury. Yet I also insisted that Baker's death was an anomaly in our small town. Wasn't drug abuse honestly more of a city problem, in places like Rutland? Irritatingly, though, the DOL kept emailing reminders to sign up, so I finally capitulated and enrolled in an upcoming training in Burlington, Vermont's largest city. I needed the continuing ed credits anyway.

Sprawled along Lake Champlain, Burlington's metropolitan area lies sixty miles from my house in Hardwick. In early April, I hoped that the Queen City, with its somewhat more temperate lake climate, would offer a tease of the season's first pink and magenta fruit tree blossoms. But Burlington's palette was as muddy and brown as Hardwick.

Shortly before nine, I parked my Toyota on top of a parking garage near Burlington's public library. I pulled on my coat and hat, tightened my scarf around my neck, and peered over the cement half wall. Whitecaps roiled the slate-hued lake.

Disappointed at the blustery weather — so much for the leisurely stroll I'd anticipated along the waterfront after the workshop — I chose a seat toward the back of the library's meeting room and flipped through the fat packet laid out on the table.

A tall man in a crisp violet dress shirt and pin-striped slacks began the presentations by introducing himself as an alcoholic in recovery. "I used to think I was just a bad dude, a weak-willed guy, a terrible person. Another person can have one drink and enjoy it — or not have that drink and still be satisfied. But for me, that one drink always turned into two, and then three, and then a whole bottle. My body has no stopping point for drinking. I just drink. Now I know it's not all within my control. My genes are a piece of my problem, too."

On my packet, I wrote "genes" and "addiction" and marked a black box around each word.

"Last summer, my neighborhood had a block party, a barbecue night. A neighbor asked me to have a drink. 'Come on, just one beer.' I said, 'No thanks, man.' The neighbor kept teasing me. 'Come on,' he said, 'it's one beer.' I told him that he didn't understand. That for me 'one beer' was an impossibility. That one beer would lead to six, and six would lead to twelve, and I would go down the hole again that took me years to climb out of."

I envisioned the presenter, in shorts and a T-shirt, standing on his sidewalk on a hot July afternoon, music blaring and kids circling on bikes and splashing in plastic wading pools, BBQ smoke permeating the air. Booze was everywhere. Coolers held stashes of beer cans, and opened bottles of gin and vodka and whiskey were clustered on picnic tables in makeshift bars.

A woman with a fat silver topknot looked up from her yellow legal pad where she was writing copious cursive notes. "Did he understand what you meant?"

"He did not. In his world, he can drink one beer. For me to keep drinking might seem like a personal failing. I should be able to just stop. But I know now, and this took me years to learn — I'll emphasize that again, years, folks — that I can't stop once I've started. My genes are inescapable. The only thing I can do is not take that first drink."

The woman tapped her pen tip on the pad. "That seems fairly straightforward. Don't take that first drink."

The presenter laughed. "Ma'am, I assure you, there is nothing straightforward about it. Learning not to drink cost me my marriage, two jobs, my house, and almost my son."

His warm baritone tugged me in and made me want to laugh with him, but his confession startled me. How had I not realized that genetics held trump cards in addiction? Behind a mask of respectability, I had for years concealed my own demon. But now I wondered: genes and addiction? I'm a librarian, after all. Hadn't I read anything?

Beyond those two words — *genes* and *addiction* — the page in front of me was blank. I flipped my pen around and around in one hand, stuck on a question I was trying to form. Finally, I raised my hand. "Would you say you now have the upper hand on alcohol? That you beat your addiction?"

"I'll never best addiction. It's here." He tapped his chest. "But what I have learned is how to live with it. I've learned not to take that first drink. I can stand in my neighborhood and tell my neighbor I can't drink. I can admit I had a problem and lost — and lost almost everything. Understanding my genetic composition helps me accept that alcohol and me are a poisonous combination. I now see my addiction as a disease, one I'll always have. Does that answer your question?"

I nodded.

During the next presentation about social service agencies and programs for people in recovery, my eyes kept drifting back to the first presenter. He listened attentively, legs crossed, one shiny wing tip bouncing. If I had met him somewhere else, I never would have guessed that he was also a former drinker. Then again, how many of my patrons knew my history?

In the last presentation, a woman from a prevention agency held up a small white box in each hand. "This saves lives. Everyone should carry it, because you never know when you'll have a chance to save someone's life." Narcan isn't difficult to use, she explained. Just stick it up the person's nose.

A thin woman in a long green rayon dress lifted her hand. "Great presentation. I so appreciate this. I didn't realize I would get an education this morning, in addition to the Narcan. I wish my trustee chair had come with me. She's adamantly opposed to keeping Narcan in the library. She insists that's what the rescue squad is for."

"Look," the preventionist responded, "someone can die from an overdose in minutes. That's all it takes for drugs to shut down a body irretrievably. Before we had Narcan, we saw a young woman die on our office floor, even though we are located just minutes from the city fire department. If we'd had Narcan then, that young woman might be alive today. You can bet we have it now. If for no other reason, keep it on hand so your staff — God forbid — will never have to stand there and watch someone die." When she finished speaking, she seemed out of breath, panting somewhat, as if she had been running. "Any other questions?"

There were none.

When the session ended, I collected my two boxes and stashed them in my backpack. Still pondering the link between those two words I had outlined, *genes* and *addiction*, I skipped the post-presentation chit-chat I usually relished, the tidbits about favorite new reads and fresh gossip, like who had found a handgun in their library bathroom. As I hurried through the library's front door, the woman in the green dress appeared beside me and grabbed my elbow. "You dropped this." She held out my scarf.

"Thank you!" I pressed the scarf to my face and breathed in our lavender-scented laundry soap. Worn with use, the gray cotton, rippled with faded blue stripes, was soft as milkweed fluff. In warm and cold seasons, I had used this scarf for so many years I no longer remembered its origin. Maybe from a box of hand-me-downs my cousin had mailed, or from the lost-and-found box I frequently raided in college?

I left town without stopping at any of my favorite Burlington haunts. I skipped browsing through the Crow Bookshop or dashing into City Market to stock up on their homemade chorizo and buy a cup of their strong coffee to sip on my way home. As I followed Route 2 along the twisting Winooski River, I kept glancing at the white boxes of Narcan on the passenger seat and thinking about John Baker. Narcan wouldn't have saved his life. But what might have?

In Woodbury, I stopped by the library to drop off the boxes of Narcan. The library doesn't have much storage — not even coat hooks — so I buried the boxes in a cabinet behind loose-leaf folders of outdated interlibrary loan records. At my desk, I checked the phone messages and noted two requested book renewals. On a whim, before I left, I dialed up the North Central Vermont Recovery Center, a few miles away in Morrisville. When a woman answered on the third ring, I fumbled. "Hi . . . I'm the librarian in Woodbury. I'm, well, I'm looking for information."

"We have plenty of info here. Are you looking for a schedule of meetings or a list of services?"

"Well . . . I'm actually wondering about opioid abuse, generally. Maybe how someone starts using opioids? And what might help them quit?"

"Those are big questions."

I sighed. "I know. I'm not entirely sure what it is I'm asking, or what I want to know."

"Why don't you come in and talk with me? My name is Meg Goulet. I'm in recovery, and I often share my story."

"You'd just talk with me?"

"Of course. That's what I do."

We made a date to meet the following week. I thanked her, then hung up, and immediately regretted agreeing to meet her. A single mom working two jobs, I have little spare time. Unlike attending the presentation that morning, which earned me continuing ed credits, I'd be speaking with Meg off the payroll.

It's an hour, I thought. *That's all. Go ahead and meet her for an hour.*

∾

Driving to meet Meg, I passed the Morrisville McDonald's with its popular drive-through window, a cluster of gas stations, and a Dunkin' Donuts. In addition to the small-town standards — a handful of restaurants and bars, a movie theater, the ubiquitous office buildings — the town boasts the region's only hospital and a fair-sized nursing home. When I first moved to the area two decades ago, white chickens wandered beside a ramshackle farmhouse along the busy highway. Now both house and hens are gone. Industrial parks, box stores, and strip malls have supplanted the dooryard and hayfields.

On my countless treks to Morrisville for groceries or the ski-and-bike shop for gear or bike repairs, I had often driven by the North Central Vermont Recovery Center on the main highway, Route 100. The center's vivid sign depicts silhouetted people and Vermont's emblematic cow standing on a blue-and-green Earth, surrounded by a warm yellow glow. Arriving early there that morning, I dawdled before I went in, wandering around the building and into the side yard, where the center caretakes a number of raised garden beds. The soil had been turned over recently and prepped for seed. On a picnic table, a metal can was filled with sand and stubbed-out ciga-rette butts. I worried that this woman I hadn't met would be touchy-feely or too eager to make a connection. I wasn't interested in that. I simply wanted answers to my questions — like, what was the attraction of opioids?

At precisely 9:00 a.m., I breathed in deeply and forced myself to open the front door. In the first room, a man with a neatly trimmed blond beard stood up from a chair in one corner and flashed a smile so kind that I was instantly relieved. "I'm here to meet Meg," I said.

"Sure. I'll get her."

The sunny waiting room reminded me of the Planned Parenthood in Brattleboro that I frequented when I was a college student. The clinic was located on the first floor of a converted house, its waiting room cozy with baskets of toys, a child-sized table and chairs, and an overflowing bookshelf. The staff knew my name, and, from the way they gently joshed one another, I guessed they enjoyed working there. Slipping into a déjà vu reverie, I inhabited my single young womanhood again, walking up the wide steps of that house's veranda and reaching for the front door's oversized worn brass knob when — at the recovery center — I suddenly heard a low voice say, "Good morning, I'm Meg."

I stood and shook her outstretched hand. "I'm Brett. Thanks for meeting with me. I was just admiring the garden beds outside."

Dressed in gold pants and a sleeveless shirt on that balmy morn-ing, Meg reminded me of the Saint-John's-wort flowers blooming behind my house, a medicinal plant used for centuries to alleviate numerous maladies, including depression. "Every day, spring is out a little more. I'm loving it."

"It's a happy season."

"That's so true." She waved her hand around the room. "So this is our space. I'll give you a brief tour first." Meg showed me the public computers where folks can sit down and scroll through Facebook, the always-warm coffeepot, the salty popcorn, the donated bread and pastries and the hot bar food from Hannaford's, a local supermarket.

No charge. No requested donation. No need to talk or participate. Just show up.

After the tour, she led me to a room and closed the door. The space was sunny and decorated with framed artwork and comfortable, cushioned chairs. Meg, who appeared to be in her thirties, asked me to tell her a little bit about myself and why I had come.

"I'm a librarian — I think I mentioned that. I suspected a local man who lived nearby was using heroin. He made me realize how little I know about opioids."

"He lived nearby? Is he in rehab?"

I bit my lower lip, hard, then said, "He committed suicide."

"I see," Meg said slowly.

"I keep wondering if I should, or even if I could, have done something more."

"You probably know that, generally, someone has to want help before they accept it."

"I do. Maybe, really, what I'm trying to understand is why someone would use heroin."

"I share my story — my own 'why' — with a lot of people, in many settings. It's part of my job here, as a recovery coach, but also part of my own recovery process. Is that what you're looking for? Would that be helpful?"

"Absolutely. I've never spoken with anyone who's used opioids."

"Okay." Meg tucked her long hair behind her ears. "Well, when I lead groups, I usually begin with an icebreaker by going around the room and asking people to share one thing no one would guess about them. The point is, there's plenty more to our lives than addiction. I usually start and say that I have three titanium plates and thirteen screws in my head from a rebuilt eye socket."

Scrutinizing her, I noticed the slightest lack of muscular strength above one eye, a barely perceptible sag. I never would have guessed that metal was hidden in her body.

"Another question I sometimes ask is what people wanted to be when they were five years old. A garbageman, someone will answer.

Or an astronaut. A country-and-western singer. But I've never met anyone who wanted to grow up and struggle with addiction."

I had a sudden vision of myself at five, running barefoot over a lush lawn in Boulder, Colorado.

Meg said, "My father is an alcoholic. Friday nights while he drank, the waitress always loaded up my Shirley Temple with lots of cherries. I'm sure she felt sorry for me. I was the only kid in the bar." When she was twelve, she and a friend stole her dad's beer. "I think it was more to see if anybody would notice. I did a lot of stuff like that, like biking around town for hours, waiting to see if anybody would come looking for me." As a teenager, Meg smoked weed and drank a bit, but stayed away from harder stuff. At sixteen, she lived in a tent by herself at the Cliffs, a spot in St. Johnsbury known as the party place. St. Johnsbury, a town with a rough reputation, lies about forty minutes from Woodbury on the New Hampshire border.

"You were living in a tent?"

She shrugged. "It was summer."

"How did you get money? What about food?"

"My friend and I would go 'spanging.'" She put the word in air quotes.

"Spanging?"

"Spare changing. Panhandling. We had a daily goal — maybe it was around four dollars — for a McDonald's special they had then — two cheeseburgers, fries, and a drink. That was breakfast, lunch, and dinner, in one meal." One corner of her mouth bent up wryly. "I'm not saying it was a good plan."

I imagined two pretty young girls, giggling and feeling clever for having found a way around the rules I followed — go to school, get a job. But I reminded myself that Meg wasn't only panhandling; she was also shacked up in a tent. Living outside during a Vermont summer means rain and biting insects. She had been only sixteen, and no one was looking out for her. What did she do about guys who got drunk during those parties? A tent didn't have a door that locked. But I didn't ask.

After that summer at the Cliffs, she moved in with a friend's parents and got her GED.

"But you weren't yet using heroin?"

"Not then. To me, heroin was the worst thing, even though all my friends were doing it. *I'm bad*, I thought, *but I'm not that bad*."

"Even then, as a teenager, you knew you had some kind of drug problem?"

"Oh, yeah. I went to my first Narcotics Anonymous meeting when I was sixteen. Granted, I got high afterward."

"Did you go back?"

Meg laughed. "Once. The next time I made sure to get high before the meeting. But that was it. I wasn't interested in sitting around talking about drugs. I wanted to do them."

"So why did you start using heroin? Was there one particular thing that pushed you toward it?"

She tucked her hair behind her ears, then wound her fingers together and clasped one of her knees, gazing at the floor.

While I waited for her answer, I studied a painting hung on the wall behind her of a white iris blossom, its petals open, disarrayed as if the flower had been tossed in a windstorm.

Without looking at me, Meg continued. "I'd always known there was something wrong with me. When I was eight, I was raped over a five-month period by my dad's then girlfriend's son. He was thirteen or fourteen. I'd come home from staying there, and I'd be sick, throwing up or running a fever. But I don't think I would have said anything, even if I had the words. My mom never asked what was wrong, but she could tell something was going on with me, so she put me in counseling. It didn't help. After that, I knew there was something wrong with me. It just seemed to me that getting high filled that. Or fixed that. Or shut that off."

I stared at that pearly iris and the stark black background. Later in the summer, irises would bloom in clusters around my front yard, their flouncy petals far tougher than they appeared, sturdy enough to withstand hailstorms. Once, I'd offered to divide a clump for a friend's garden. When I unearthed a shovelful of tuberous roots, worms and centipedes twisted through the clumped, pebbled soil. Above that hidden realm, all spring blossoms drink in sun and rain. Those transplanted irises survived.

✿

"About this," Meg said, touching her forehead above her eyes. "The accident was my turning point." On a slushy New Year's Eve, Meg was riding in the backseat of a car when the driver announced an upcoming stop at a gas station for snacks. Wanting to be ready with her wallet, she unbuckled her seat belt to reach for her backpack while the car was moving. At full speed, the car collided with a garbage truck. When she hit the windshield, her orbital socket shattered. During the post-accident haze, Meg didn't realize how badly she was injured. In the hospital at some point, unwilling to wait for a nurse to help her to the bathroom, she went alone and glimpsed her reflection in a mirror. "I started screaming. I had two black eyes and stitches and cuts everywhere. I looked and felt like a monster."

I winced. "You were still sixteen?"

"Yeah. The accident was horrible, but the healing was, too." To stimulate the nerves and encourage blood flow, she was instructed to place hot sandbags on her face. But no one told her that her face was unable to sense heat, and the sandbags burned her skin. "My big bottle of pain medication got rid of the physical pain, but also all the emotional pain, the mental pain. It just numbed me. I didn't understand why everybody did not have this magic bottle with them. That magic fixed everything."

Gone was the sulky teenager who thought "spanging" was cool. I imagined a girl with a mangled, painful face. Fuck, I would have taken the meds, too.

✿

"There's more," she said. "Do you want to hear it, or have you had enough?"

"Go on, if you want to. I'd like to know how you quit using."

"I got worse before I got better. The legal prescription ran out — as it does for so many people — and I started looking in other places. I found a crowd who supplied me with black-market pills." Sunlight streamed in through the window, glinting off the diamond ring on her slender left hand, moving in and out of her long hair.

By the time she was eighteen, Meg's injuries had healed. Though she still partied, she had a job, and "for a while things were good." She made it sound like she was asking a question — had her life ever really been good? Then she got pregnant; the baby's father pressured her to have an abortion. He and her parents "kind of ganged up" on her. "I don't care what anyone else does, but an abortion wasn't something I could do." When she insisted on keeping the baby, the boyfriend broke up with her. Behind her back, Meg's mother contacted a couple in Maine who were desperate to adopt an infant. "The adoption was pushed on me."

Meg was nineteen when she delivered the baby at the birthing center where I had my daughters. At the hospital, her mother and father bickered. In a strange conjunction of events, Meg's grandmother, just after learning the baby was born, passed away in her sleep. Meanwhile, the couple drove down from Maine to collect the baby. Meg saw her mother holding the baby in the hospital nursery and crying. "I was so mad. I was like, 'I don't want to do this. I feel all this pressure, and you're in there holding her and crying. How do you have a right to be upset?'" In the family photo her parents requested — just one, her mother pleaded — Meg said she had "the worst" look on her face. "It was a 'screw you' look."

"How did the adoption work? I mean, did someone show up in your room and whisk the baby away?"

"No, it wasn't like that at all. Since the adoption was private, I had to sign out both of us. I carried her down the elevator and out of the hospital, where I met the couple from Maine in the parking lot."

Wordlessly, she stretched out her arms and showed me how she had given away her brand-new, five-pound daughter.

The night after my daughter Molly was born in that same birthing center, a nurse urged me to leave her in the nursery so I could get some sleep. Though she promised to bring Molly back when she woke and cried for milk, I insisted on keeping my baby tucked in beside me. I had labored so hard to bring this rosy-lipped little being into the world. I imagined young Meg, her body sore from child-birth, holding her infant in the elevator, maybe wondering all the ride down if this might yet end differently, if the couple from Maine might not appear, if she might still leave the parking lot with her baby.

"Then I went to the courthouse to finish signing the paperwork where the judge said what a fine, upstanding young man the baby's father was, since he had joined the military. I was so angry." Afterward, she traveled to Massachusetts for her grandmother's funeral. "My family doesn't talk about things. Our attitude is, *It's over. It's done. Move on.* Things kind of went downhill from there."

In just a few years, so much had happened to Meg — a terrible car accident, an unplanned pregnancy, a coerced adoption. "Moving on" must have seemed impossible.

"From there, I started going back to things I had been doing before, but even more so."

While pregnant, she hadn't used substances. After the adoption, she started drinking again and returned to the magic pills' soothing numbness. Then, nearly two years to the day after her oldest daughter was born, Meg had another baby — a second chance. She was determined to keep this child. But though she sobered up during pregnancy, soon after the baby was born, Meg's relationship with her second baby's father failed, too. "I don't really know what led me back down to trouble. But I did go down. I definitely did." One day, she ran out of pills and someone offered her heroin. She told herself that snorting wasn't the same as shooting up — "it's bad, but it's not that bad." Not long after, she began injecting heroin. "The list of things I said I'd never do got shorter and shorter until there was no list left at all."

Though the afternoon sun had warmed the room, I suddenly felt chilled. Wrapping my scarf around my shoulders, I curled up my legs underneath me and sank further into the deep chair.

At her family's urging, Meg checked into rehab at the Brattleboro Retreat, while her daughter stayed with Meg's mother and the girl's father. For a few years, Meg drifted in and out of treatment. She'd come home and be good for a month, or two months, or six months, and then something would happen.

"So you'd get clean for a while, but then start using again?"

"Right. We call relapse random, but it's not. All the things you've never dealt with have a way of creeping back up, and you just want to numb out again. I knew I didn't want to do what I was doing anymore, but I didn't really know how to stop. I had this unrealistic expectation that a wave of a fairy rehab wand should fix me."

During one of her sober periods, Meg sequestered herself in her apartment to keep from temptation. One day a former boyfriend called and said he had quit using, too. He was driving to St. Albans and asked if she wanted to ride along. "I was so lonely that I thought, *Why not?* If he wasn't using, what was the risk? But when we got on the interstate, he threw a bag of heroin on my lap and that was it."

During those years, she drove countless trips south on Interstate 91 to Hartford, Connecticut, for cheaper drugs; prices are considerably higher in Vermont, as the supply is less plentiful. Eventually, she was pulled over in Brattleboro and charged with possession of eighty-eight bags of heroin. She left the police station that night with a little pink piece of paper. Despite the severity of the potential consequences, the charge didn't seem real. Broke and marooned in Brattleboro, she phoned her mother and begged her to wire money, fabricating a story that her car had been impounded after she parked in a forbidden zone. It was Christmas Eve. "I wanted desperately to get home and find somebody who would give me something. Which I did."

A few days later, her mother called, infuriated. Meg's arrest and charges had been broadcast on the local news channel. The problem was, in fact, so real she couldn't ignore it any longer. In an attempt to avoid jail, Meg agreed to check herself back into the Brattleboro Retreat. After two weeks, she expected to be released but was transferred instead to Valley Vista, an addiction treatment center in Bradford, Vermont, that had space for her. During the sixty-three days she spent there, her landlords, who had also seen the news footage, sent her an eviction notice, and she lost custody of her four-year-old daughter. "Everything in my life fell apart. But still, there was no lightbulb for me. No aha moment. If anything, I wanted to use more. Because, really, I figured, what's the point of not using?"

Luckily for Meg, the judge ordered probation instead of prison time and instructed her to enroll in an intensive outpatient program three days a week, for three hours a day. Terrified of going to jail, Meg didn't use. "But I promised myself, *The day I get off probation, I'll start again.* A lot of my time, honestly, was spent with my middle finger in the air, saying, 'Screw you, everybody.'" But when probation ended, a week passed and she realized she was still sober.

"You're saying quitting wasn't a conscious decision?"

"Not really."

"But something must have changed in you."

She sighed. "Yes and no. A lot of it was just my stubbornness and my wanting to prove my daughter's father wrong. He kept insisting, 'Once a fuckup, always a fuckup.'"

As part of her recovery work, she enrolled in classes at the local community college and started volunteering at the recovery center, which morphed into a job.

"I was expecting to hear that you experienced some kind of revelation, but your recovery sounds like it was step by step?"

"I didn't see a sudden, blinding light, if that's what you're asking."

"I guess that's what I'm asking."

"My recovery was slow. People who know me know that I have a thing about quotes, and one of my favorites is, 'New beginnings are often disguised as painful endings.'"

"That's pithy. Sometimes those painful endings appear like locked doors, in my experience — like divorce, in my case."

"Right. Or adoption."

"What about your older daughter? Were you able to have any contact with her?"

She nodded. "I'd always sent birthday cards and gifts, but I'd only seen her once. Last June, she invited me to her high school graduation. So I went."

"What was it like?"

Meg moaned. "So complex. So painful. I know she's had a great life, and I'm so grateful for that. But the adoption is still so hard for me. If I had made the decision on my own and that was what I wanted . . ." Her voice ebbed, and she closed her eyes. "Acceptance has been really hard. Let's just put it that way."

I grimaced. "I'm so very sorry."

"My oldest came to my wedding that summer, too. She kept thanking me for everything and asking for one more hug. I said, 'Hon, you have nothing to thank me for.' She looked at me and said, 'I have everything to thank you for.'"

In my lap, my fists twisted together.

"If I hadn't done the work, if I hadn't made those changes, we would never have shared that moment. I would never have been in a place where I would have wanted her to meet me."

I winced, feeling the pain of self-appraisal. That place of reckoning was familiar.

"Before you leave, I want you to know that working at the recovery center and being able to help other people is powerful. I recently did a presentation at Valley Vista in Bradford. One guy gave me a weird look the whole time. At a break, he came up to me and said,

'You're telling me I just wasted the last nine years of my life?' He'd been in the Brattleboro Retreat when I was there the last time. We had similar legal troubles, similar family dynamics, similar addictions. He went one way, and I went another."

She stretched her left hand out into the sunlight and flipped it over, as if she were looking into the palm of her empty hand. The diamonds on her ring finger scattered a shower of tiny rainbows over the wall.

"So that was kind of weird. He's checked into Valley Vista, and I'm giving the presentation."

ℳ

Together we walked down the hall. Meg stopped at a table and picked up a handful of pamphlets about the center for me to take back to the library. Through the open doorway, I saw that the front room was beginning to fill with people chatting, sitting, or leaning against walls.

"Thank you again for sharing your story with me," I said. "I learned so much this morning."

"Hey," she said, shrugging, "that's what we do here. We share."

A man called across the room, "Morning, Meg!"

"Morning, Jimmy!" Then, lowering her voice, she told me, "The thing is, when I was in the worst place, I honestly thought that the people who were in recovery — people who had a week, a month, a year — had something that I didn't have. I tried so hard. I thought for sure there was a piece missing in me. But there wasn't. And there isn't for anyone else. That's what I want people to know. That's what I wish I had known."

I slipped the pamphlets into my backpack.

A young woman rushed up and embraced Meg. "I heard you got married!"

I stepped away, waved good-bye to Meg, mouthed, *Thank you!* and walked out.

A sudden wind whirled through the parking lot, driving sand into my blinking eyes. Fat, coal-streaked clouds clustered over the roof of the recovery center, a sure sign of approaching rain. On Route 100, a black SUV with four adolescent girls drove by. In the backseat, one girl stuck her head out the window and shouted, "Fuck you!" at a shirtless teenage boy biking on the sidewalk. In reply, he raised one tattooed arm with an extended middle finger. Across the busy highway, the Lamoille River bent around the town's athletic field, where shoots of shimmering green were emerging through last year's dead, brown grass. In the center of the field, preschoolers tossed a red Frisbee. One tiny girl leaned her head back and lifted her face to the sky, her mouth wide open in joy or frustration; I stood too far away to know.

If I had met teenage Meg a few days ago walking down the street in Burlington, "spanging" me for nickels and quarters, I would have hurried by. But what would I have known about her life, really? For that matter, what had I really known about John Baker?

A hot wind sifted dirt over my teeth and tongue. I swallowed, suddenly thirsty, and glanced back at the recovery center where people were milling around on the other side of the glass door. Rain began in drips. Inhaling the musty scent of the storm rapidly moving in, I gazed up at the thunderheads racing across the sky. As the clouds broke, dumping rain, I hurried to my car. For a few minutes, I stared through the blurry windshield, thinking of that glittering ring — Meg's rainbow.

four

Neighbors

On an unusually warm spring Sunday when the daffodils' petals had begun to wither at their edges, Gabriela hurried into the kitchen. Blond wispy hair at the nape of her neck, damp from her morning run, curled below her double French braids. "Why's the lower barn door open? None of us have been down there all winter."

I scraped chopped onions off my cutting board into a boiling pot of pinto beans. *That's not good*, I thought. A small chunk of wood secured the door. The block rotated on a nail hammered on the inside of the door frame and couldn't open by itself.

While Vermont is famous for its enormous red hay barns, ours is a small carriage-house. A ramp leads into the main floor where we keep the mower, bicycles, lawn chairs, and things the girls have outgrown — like a once-beloved doll stroller — but I can't bear to relinquish. The barn's basement is cut into the hillside and has a damp cement floor lined with rows of double-decker wire chicken cages built by a previous owner. A low roof slants over the barn's third floor. At the back end, a single window frames a view of box elder branches. A covered porch connects the barn and house.

Gabriela waited. She was the child who, at three, pinched her lips together, distressed but not crying, after a blackberry thorn scraped a thin bloody scratch across the shin. "I don't like to be opened up," she told me. Now she twirled a small curl around her finger.

"I'm sure it's nothing," I said. "Let's go have a look."

She followed me outside.

I walked through the yard, around the scraggly crab apple tree I had recently planted, and behind the barn. Down the slope behind my compost pile, tiger lilies shot up pale green sprouts.

The barn's back window had been shattered, the wooden frame snapped into splinters, as if by a baseball bat. I crouched in last year's dead grass, gingerly extracting shards of glass with my thumb and forefingers.

Behind me, Gabriela murmured, "Whoa. Thieves. And I thought the wind blew the door open."

I piled the jagged glass pieces on the unbroken sill.

She ran into the barn through the open door. More cautiously, looking around, I followed her into the dim basement, which smelled of musty, damp straw. Empty flower pots were stacked unevenly in a corner beside a lopsided wicker settee I had gleaned from a roadside free pile last fall.

From upstairs, Gabriela shouted to me, "They took the tires."

"What? The tires?" I hurried up the narrow staircase. On the main floor, the summer tires for my car and Molly's Honda — eight in all — were missing. In two stacks, they had dominated the barn all winter. We had intended to swap them for our studded snow tires that coming week.

On the third floor, Gabriela hollered, "They left the camping gear!"

I walked around the cluttered main level. My grandmother's wing chair was piled with cardboard boxes of donations for the library's used-book sale. Our recycling bin, filled with empty cat food cans and smashed pasta boxes, overflowed near the door. The cardboard cat house my daughter created three years ago sagged in a back corner, its roof pasted with white paper plates for shingles. Who had been in our barn, wandering around our trash and recycling, my tires in their hands?

Gabriela stood at the top of the stairs, eyebrows raised. "Only the tires?"

"Looks like it."

"You have to call the police."

"I know."

I walked outside and stood at the edge of our lawn. A century ago, during Hardwick's granite quarrying heyday, our two-story house was built at the end of a short street that ends at a town cemetery.

Evenings, when we walk across the village and up Bridgeman Hill to admire the sunset, we can see our house across the valley — white clapboards, windows shiny with the dwindling sunlight, the barn's red metal roof. Behind our yard, tangles of honeysuckle and black-berry brambles surround a footpath connecting the cemetery with a mobile home park down the slope from us. In our kitchen at night, I can see only a single light glowing through the woods, the foliage dense year round with evergreens.

Holding my phone in one hand, I studied the layout of our house, barn, and the path down to the trailer park. On the other side of the rusting chain-link fence, a skinny old woman in a buttoned-up quilted blue coat walked her two fluffy-tailed golden retrievers.

I dialed the Hardwick Police Department, explained that I had been robbed, and asked if someone could come out. "Sure thing, ma'am."

Within minutes, an officer drove up in a cruiser and got out. "Great spot on the hill." He leaned back on his heels, hands on his lean hips, appraising my house behind black sunglasses. My dresses and T-shirts hung on the clothesline strung across the porch. "I used to watch fireworks up here as a kid. My buddy's grandma lived in this house, and — man! — what a view of the sky. House wasn't as kept up then. Looks like the porch has been completely replaced, huh? Covered at one end? That's smart."

"The previous owners rebuilt it. So our back window . . ."

The officer followed me behind the barn.

I pointed to the broken glass. "What do you think?"

"Yeah, that's no soccer ball. Looks like we're talking about a break-in."

"I think this happened last night."

The officer lifted a piece of the broken window sash and held it between us. "Looks like they came prepared. Surprised you didn't hear anything."

"Our house is well insulated. Plus, there are no bedroom windows on the back."

Crouching with the jagged wood in his hand, the officer twisted around to look up at me. I couldn't see his eyes behind his dark glasses. "You lived here long?"

"A couple of years."

"Before that?"

"Woodbury, for a long time."

"But you're not from around here?"

"No. Does that matter?"

He stood up. "Let's take a walk, huh?"

I followed the officer across my yard. At my garden, we turned and walked along the path to the mobile home park through the thorny brambles and down into the thicket of pines. There the path dropped steeply. Where the path ended at the pavement, he crouched and lifted a dirty, twisted white plastic bag inked with the light blue Goodyear logo. "This yours?"

"Looks like one of the bags our tires were in. Evidence?"

He shrugged. "I'll put out the word, see if we can find those tires, but it's not likely. Honestly, ma'am, I'd put up cameras. Everyone's doing it these days." The officer looked at his watch. "I have to head out — sorry I'm in such a rush — but call the station if you have more difficulties." He turned around and headed back up the hill to his car.

I shook out the crumpled, torn plastic, then knotted the bag around a branch.

"Jerks," I muttered. I stared down at the neighborhood of mobile homes. So early on a Sunday morning, no one was outside.

∽

I walked slowly back to our house. By the time I arrived, the cruiser had left, and my daughters were strapping their kayaks to the roof rack of Molly's Honda. "Cameras," Molly said. Wiry in skinny jeans, she stepped back from her car and clapped her hands clean. "That's what he told us to get."

My oldest is a few inches taller than her younger sister, but my daughters are unmistakably sisters, graced with similar faces and different personalities. Molly chatters steadily; Gabriela silently appraises.

I said, "I heard about the cameras. You're headed where?"

"Nichols Pond." Molly opened the back door and loaded in the paddles. "We already researched and added a few suggestions to your Amazon cart."

"Already? That's fast."

"We did it while you were wandering around. Come on, cameras are an obvious solution."

I picked up the life jackets from the grass and tossed them on the backseat. "I don't know. Am I trying to start a gated community?"

"What is your problem with cameras?"

"It's an invasion of privacy."

She laughed. "Whose privacy are you protecting? The thieves'? Hello? Robbers are bad news."

"Fine. I'll buy the cameras. Have a good trip. Don't forget to bring your life jackets in the kayaks with you."

Gabriela groaned.

"Just do it. Please. You don't have to wear them. Humor me."

⁂

After the girls left, I dragged out the rickety wicker settee and read *Where the Crawdads Sing* for a while, but I kept losing track of the plot. Eventually, I closed the book and decided to take a walk and clear my head.

When I reached the cemetery, I stopped to tie my shoelace. Through the trees — not yet leafed out — I saw the upper tier of the mobile home park. A man in a gray hoodie stood on a small, square deck in front of a white trailer, talking on a cell phone and gesturing with his other arm. By the corner of his deck, I spied a stack of tires. I remained crouched down so he wouldn't see me and strained to hear what he was saying.

A few stray words rang clear: "dog" and "thought" and "told you."

The trailer door opened, and a shirtless young man walked out, rubbing his eyes.

The man on the phone called out. "Yo! Who's up early?"

The shirtless man turned around and disappeared back inside.

Early? I thought. It was well past lunchtime.

I counted four tires in the stack, with a fifth leaning against the pile, next to a full-sized refrigerator, its door ajar.

That skinny old woman with the golden retrievers appeared around the bend, hustling up the path toward me. I tightened my shoelace and stood up. Passing, she gave me a single nod.

As I was heading home, my phone rang, the number of my brother, Nik, flashing across its screen. I stopped beneath a tree to talk. "Hello?"

"What kind of crime zone are you living in these days? Your kids left me a message about security cameras."

"Someone smashed our back barn window and stole our tires. It's probably a freak, onetime thing — or I hope it is, at least."

"Yeah, well, things get stolen."

"That's why I sold our old house and moved."

"Speaking of that — any chance your crazy ex is breaking in again?"

"I don't know. Maybe. It's not like the robbers left a note. 'Hey, thanks for the tires. Pick up the messy recycling next time.'"

Nik laughed. "But seriously, buy the cameras. And replace those tires. I'll send you money."

"We're fine; I'm working. I keep thinking of how Eric broke into our house, so many times. I'd come home from work and find little things awry — a missing block of cheddar cheese from our refrigerator or a tincture bottle he dropped. Never that 'hard evidence' the police needed." I reached the edge of our lawn, overlooking my vegetable garden. That week, the garlic had poked tender nubs through the matted straw mulch.

"I get it. You're afraid. But try not to scare the kids, okay?"

"Okay. But I'm still mad."

"Go ahead. Be mad. But don't be stupid."

⁓

That evening, after dinner, we stood on the back porch listening to the robins trill, eating chocolate chip cookies Gabriela had baked that afternoon. I reached over a railing and tugged on a lilac bush twig. "Look at this." Gently, I rubbed my thumb over a plump green bud. "What would you guess? You think the blossoms will open by the end of May?" The white, lavender, and deep purple flowers surround our house on three sides. When they bloom, our house is wreathed, day and night, in their marvelous perfume.

"May seems like forever from now," Gabriela said. She went back inside to work on her soccer scrapbook.

"You want to know my plan about my fall classes?" Molly asked.

"Tell me while we walk into the cemetery. We can check out the sunset."

"Okay." She slid on her flip-flops, and we headed down the path. "I'm thinking I'll take the first semester of Anatomy and Physiology in the fall, then the second semester in the spring. I have to get an A. I want the professor to write me a recommendation. He has a really good rep, and that should go a long way toward getting me into nursing school. Do you know there's seventy-nine kinds of skin? Or something like that. What are you looking at? You're not listening to me."

We had stopped near a metal trash can overflowing with artificial flowers, broken and sun-faded.

"I didn't realize how easy it is to see through there, when the leaves aren't out yet." I pointed down the hill toward the deck with the pile of tires. A silver pickup was parked in the drive.

"You think those people broke in our barn?"

"Maybe."

"For all you know, those tires have been there for years. Since when did you ever spot-check the neighbors' junk?"

Through the trees, I scrutinized the square deck and column of tires.

Molly stepped back from me. "I went to school with a lot of kids who live there. Some of them couldn't believe I actually live in a real house — not an apartment, not a trailer. What do you think they think of us, living up here?"

"I get that. But I don't want to be robbed. How do you think your sister feels? She's home alone a lot."

"You're buying cameras, right? If they come back, they'll get caught."

I imagined strangers bumping around our barn in the dark, wandering by the light of cell phones. "I know you're right. I'm still pissed, though."

"How do you think we look to them? You may be a single mother, but you don't earn minimum wage. I'm going to college. I know you worked hard to get us where we are, but still, you had more to begin with."

For a few minutes, we stared through the gaps in the trees at the silver pickup, gray road, stained metal house, and stack of tires.

"Let's go," Molly said sharply.

∾

The next morning, after Gabriela waved good-bye and walked to school and Molly left for work, I phoned the police again.

I spoke with the officer who had visited the day before. "I found the receipt from the garage."

He took down my information about tire make and size. "That's helpful, ma'am."

"So, also, I think my tires may be in the trailer park. On the third tier."

"What makes you suspect that?"

"Well, I saw a stack of tires on someone's deck. A silver pickup was parked out front."

"Okay. We'll swing by."

"What does that mean?"

"It means I'll do the best I can, ma'am."

I thanked him and hung up.

On my way to work, I stopped by the co-op where I saw June Jenkins at the bulk coffee bin. Her son had been in my daughter's elementary school class, and we volunteered together in a monthly naturalist program that chaperoned class walks into the school wetlands.

"Spring!" she enthused. She tugged on the short sleeve of her violet shirt. "T-shirt weather again. The trilliums and trout lilies are out."

"So are the thieves." I briefly recapped the robbery.

"That's terrible," she commiserated. "South Woodbury and around Calais, where I am, has been hit hard by petty theft over the past few years. Tools, tires, electronics. It sucks."

"The police told me I needed to install cameras if I wanted to catch anyone."

"There's cameras everywhere around me. It's one Big Brother zone. But that's not enough. My neighbor down the road had all his power tools stolen. Police caught the guy, but the court system let him go. Turns out, Vermont isn't big on locking people up for petty theft."

"That's so irritating. I bought those tires for my daughter."

"It's outrageous. Someone has probably already traded them in for something they could shoot up."

I pulled the lever and released a stream of coffee beans into a paper bag. Finished, I taped it closed.

June said, "Good luck," and pushed her cart away.

I held the coffee bag in one hand. We had nothing of value left in the barn. What if the thieves decided to break our kitchen window next?

five

A Wounded Heart

After two stormy, overcast summers, that July was mercifully sunny. My daughters and I often swam in nearby Mackville Pond in the gloaming, before driving home to start dinner and pull in the day's dried laundry from the clothesline, our sheets and T-shirts warm with the day's sunlight. Winter in Vermont contracts into a dearth of light and color, but summer at its loveliest hums with bird and cricket songs.

In the early 1800s, Mackville was dammed to power grist, lumber, and woolen mills. While those industries have long since vanished, the dam's granite foundation survives, cordoned off by plastic orange and white balls that float, half submerged, on the water's glassy surface. All summer, kids cannonball from a cement bridge that crosses the pond near the dam. Local lore claims that Mackville is leech territory — a rumor that keeps the crowds sparse — but where we swim, off the rocky bank, we've encountered only bullfrogs and sunfish and schools of quicksilver minnows.

One Monday in mid-July, I spread my towel on the grassy bank and saw my friend Diane walking up the road from her house, a tall glass of milky iced coffee in one hand, talking with her teenage daughter Bea. Diane wore blue cotton overalls, and her hair hung to her shoulders, streaked in places with gray, like mine. When they reached the bank, Bea said hello, dropped her towel, and swam out to my daughters, who were lounging on a plastic floatie, a sun-faded orange triangle painted with a circle of pepperoni and a curl of green pepper — one of Gabriela's recent birthday presents. We called it "the pizza."

Diane handed me her glass. "Try this. I have the proportions of maple syrup, cream, and coffee just right."

I sipped the cool drink. "Perfection." A pickup passed on the road behind us, the teenage driver honking. The girls hollered and waved back. I handed the glass back to Diane and said, "Remember when the kids couldn't talk?"

"Remember when they napped?"

I laughed. "And it felt like they would be toddlers forever?"

"I miss the napping."

Diane spread her towel and sat down. I pulled out my knitting from my canvas bag. I had recently started a violet sweater, an intricate design with gold flowers along the hem.

Molly swam back, knotted a towel around her waist, and adjusted her black bikini straps. With her iPhone, she snapped photos of the thirteen-year-olds on the floatie, then asked Diane, "Mom tell you what she's been up to lately?"

My friend raised her eyebrows at me. "Did you?"

"Just the same old stuff. Buying a lot of library books. Mulching the tomatoes with straw I just bought. Eight bucks a bale — that's crazy high. Made a super-garlicky batch of pesto last night."

Molly looked at Diane. "That's not all she's been doing."

"Oh? Do tell."

"Good Lord," I said. "Let's not be dramatic."

Above us, Molly's sunglasses reflected our upturned faces in two rectangular mirrors. "She invited an addict to come to our house and talk."

Diane scrutinized me. "You know what you're doing?"

"She's been in recovery for years."

"You sold our old house because my crazy father kept breaking in. What if we start getting robbed again? Hello? Drug users and theft? What are you going to do then? Pack up and move again?"

"A conversation is not going to lead to a robbery. We're talking — that's all."

"But we got robbed this spring! Hello? My summer tires? I'm just saying . . ."

Molly walked up the road, crossed the bridge, and leaned over the metal railing. "We should get ice cream later," she said to the girls drifting on the orange floatie, arms dangling in the water.

Quietly, Diane asked, "What are you doing, anyway?"

I held up my sweater, studying the half-knit hem. "I'm not entirely sure."

My friend fingered the thin wool. "The sweater's going to be gorgeous."

"I've unraveled it multiple times already. This pattern is so hard. And I feel like it's written in a language I don't understand."

In the water, Gabriela flipped over the floatie with a huge splash and shouted at us. "Come swim!"

"In a minute!" I called back.

Dragonflies darted above the pond, their miniature wings flickering in the sunlight. Beyond the girls, the loon's ebony head poked through the calm water, then disappeared again. I wondered where the loon would emerge — nearer us, or farther down the narrow pond?

Diane said, "Be careful, okay?"

"Always." I laid my barely begun knitting project on the towel, stood up, and dove through the pollen-covered surface.

∽

A few days earlier I had emailed Jeri Wohlberg, a nurse practitioner at the Hardwick Health Center, asking for more information about opioid abuse in our area. Jeri suggested that I speak with Shauna Shepard, a medical receptionist in the clinic's office who was in recovery from opioid abuse. I wrote to Shauna, introducing myself as a local librarian. "Do you think you could help me understand substance abuse a little more deeply? In the winter, a suicide was connected with my library, and the man had been suspected of using drugs."

Shauna replied right away. She had heard news of Baker's death and added that she was open with her past and would be willing to talk. I invited her to visit a few days later, on Tuesday afternoon, when I knew Molly would be at work.

∽

Waiting on our back deck for Shauna to arrive, I knit a few more rows of that sweater, following the pattern's chart: purple, purple, purple, gold. I half hoped Shauna would stand me up, so Gabriela and I could swim. Addiction is scary — opioid use even scarier — and a part of me felt like I'd already seen enough. Maybe Molly was right — why invite in more scary stories? But I needed to figure out why I felt so damn guilty about what had happened with John Baker, a man I didn't even know.

A few minutes after five, Shauna hurried up my walkway, clutching an almost empty iced tea bottle, a packet of American Spirit cigarettes, and a bubblegum-pink lighter.

"Thank you so much for coming."

"Yeah. Sure." She held up the pack of cigarettes. "I'm gonna try not to do this."

"How about we sit on the deck? It's so nice outside." From underneath a pot of red geraniums, I slid out a chipped saucer painted with holly berries and dark green leaves and set it on the table for her to use as an ashtray.

"Appreciate it." Shauna sat down, and, to my surprise, before I had even started knitting again, plunged into the heart of her story. "Here goes. So the day this all starts, there wasn't any school. I don't know why — snow or cold. My brothers and sister and I, we were home alone with nothing to do all day. My brothers went sledding on the road. My brother actually hit the guy. He went in between the tires."

"What?" I dropped the needles and yarn in my lap. How did we get from small talk about an ashtray to a car accident?

"Yeah." With the heel of one hand, Shauna smeared the flowing tears across her cheeks.

"He was hit by a car?"

"Yeah."

"How old were you?"

"I was nine. But I wasn't there. I was in the house. My brother — the one who died — he was ten. My other brother, he was six. He saw the whole thing."

I gasped. "My God, I didn't know. I'm so sorry."

"After my brother died, we didn't talk about it. Don't be a bawl-ass, my mother kept telling us kids. It was just one less plate at the table at night." Shauna covered her eyes with one hand and cried.

∽

"I'll get some Kleenex." I hurried into the house. In the bathroom, the light poured through a high, square window above the long counter. Overhead, Gabriela's footsteps creaked the upstairs floor-boards; she was probably wondering how long it would be until we went swimming. I splashed cold water on my face, then dried my cheeks and hands slowly. *It's just one conversation*, I told myself. *That's all.*

I carried the box of Kleenex outside and set it on the table between us.

Shauna exhaled a long stream of gray smoke and jabbed out her cigarette. "The driver of the pickup truck that hit my brother? I hated that guy for a long fucking time." Years later, Shauna was working in a nearby hospital's emergency room when she saw the man's daughter. "I said, it took me a really long time to realize how much her dad's life changed that day. She told me, 'How much all of our lives changed that day.' I hadn't thought of it that way, but I real-ized, yeah, that's true. It was just bad luck. It wasn't really his fault. Like I said, my brother slid in between his tires. But I blamed that man for a really, really long time."

Shauna uncapped the bottle of sweet tea and drank, staring at the back of my barn, where the box elder branches touched the corner board. As if to herself, she remarked, with a slight shudder, "My brother's death spread out so far."

About a mile west of Hardwick village, unpaved Bunker Hill Road, where Shauna lived as a child, cuts north off Route 15 and winds up a steep hillside. Not far up this back road, a house designed by the famous architect Peter Eisenman — a cluster of connected cement boxes and glass walls — perches on a slope, with a vista of the valley and the Lamoille River below. That house is a glaring anomaly among the modest houses and trailers surrounded by woodpiles and tractors and rusting pickup trucks raided for parts.

Shauna told me about her hardworking mother and the man who was with her for years, Jared Johnson (she always referred to him by his first and last names). "He was fucking mean. He killed our fish. He kicked my brother in the ass so hard one time it dislocated his hip."

"Why was he so mean?"

She shrugged, then lit another cigarette. "I think he was just fucked up. He was abused when he was a kid." She told me how he killed one of their dogs and lied about it, claiming he sent it away. Later her sister discovered the remains of the dog's decaying body in the woods. Eventually, Shauna's mother moved her kids to a different apartment. One night, he towed her car away.

"Did she go to the police?"

"Yeah. But it didn't matter." Now Jared Johnson lives in another state, but Shauna hadn't entirely let go of him. She fantasized about writing him a letter. "I would love for him to know how much his shit's still affecting me. Is he a better person now? Has he somehow come to terms with everything he did?" She cleared her throat, staring at the pink plastic lighter she was flipping around and around in her hand. "But what the fuck happened to him to make him think all this shit was okay?"

Sitting on the kitchen windowsill, our cat's tiny gray ears flickered at the sound of Shauna's voice.

"But I loved that guy. As fucked up as that sounds, I actually have more problems with my father. Even though he sold weed out of our house, and our house got raided on my sister's birthday, Jared Johnson loved us. When my brother got hit by a car, and my dad was late to his funeral, Jared Johnson was the one who let me sit on his lap and cry."

∞

Shauna tipped her head to one side and lit another cigarette. Exhaling, she said, "In that email you sent me, you said you wanted to know why I used drugs. When I think about it — and I've had an awful lot of therapy, Jesus Christ, no shortage there — something was always around. Booze or pot or some shit. But if I'm being honest, I got sick of my heart hurting all the time. I have almost two years now that I've been sober, and I can say, goddamn, my heart hurt bad."

Shauna started drinking and smoking as a young teenager, behavior her alcoholic father encouraged, as they drank together. By high school, she and her brother were snorting his prescription Ritalin. Shauna discovered that she preferred pills, for a gauzy, feel-nothing high. She didn't want to become a "sloppy, mean drunk" like the stepmother she despised. "I wanted to get high until the point I puked, because that meant I was good for the day." When she was twenty-one, her car was repossessed. Her mother's name was on the car loan, and she demanded that Shauna "get her shit together" or get out of her life.

"What did you do? Did you get yourself together?"

"For a while, but it didn't last. I checked into rehab. That's when I got the Suboxone* prescription."

"I'm going to sound naive here, but what's Suboxone?"

---

*Taken daily, Suboxone mitigates opioid withdrawal symptoms and cravings. Although not without controversy, the medication has a record of successfully assisting with addiction treatment.

"Suboxone? It's called bup, too, or buprenorphine. It knocks the edge off opioid cravings. You know about cravings?"

"Some."

"They're crazy. Cravings are unbearable. You just want to use and use and use."

"You take Suboxone daily?"

"I did. I don't anymore."

"And it worked?"

"Yeah. I mean, it worked well enough. But using kind of snuck up on me again. I went to rehab because my mother backed me into a corner. Now I can see I didn't really intend to quit."

"What do you mean?"

"It's like this: I was doing a program and all. But I wasn't entirely sober. I'd sell a little Suboxone and use that money to buy drugs. I was cheating, but I didn't think it was a big deal."

"I see." I knew how this part of the story worked. Pretend you're not really using or drinking. Lie to yourself and say just a little bit doesn't matter — while every drink or pill feeds your demon. Countless times, I had told myself, *This is my last drink*, only to start again the next night.

"Eventually, it became a very big deal." While working nights as a receptionist at the local emergency room, Shauna realized that a coworker was high. Shauna asked her for pills, and the woman became a steady supplier. "My boyfriend's son was selling heroin in those days, too. You can see how this went down."

"I'm getting a picture. How bad did it get?"

"Bad."

"So how did you finally stop? Did you hit some tipping point?"

"Mostly, I was just fucking done. By that time, all I did was find, buy, and use drugs. That's it. Every day. Eventually, I ended up in my doctor's office, begging for help to get out."

"Like on like a random Tuesday morning or something?"

"Something like that. Honestly, that whole time is a blur. The doctor sent me to rehab again." She downed the last of her tea and tightened the cap on the empty bottle. "Detoxing — you probably don't know anything about it — is just fucking awful. But I had to get everything out of my body if I wanted to take Vivitrol."[*]

"Sorry, what is Vivitrol? And why did you want to take it?"

"Vivitrol knocks the edge off cravings but doesn't have an opioid. Suboxone works for a lot of people, but it wasn't going to work for me, because it has some opioid in it."

"And it worked?"

"It wasn't easy. The withdrawal was terrible. I was so fucking sick that I couldn't go to therapy groups. To punish me for skipping groups, they wouldn't let me smoke. Goddammit, withdrawal is bad enough. So I called my boyfriend and asked him to come pick me up. When he arrived, the lady at the rehab warned him that I would probably relapse." Shauna locked herself in her house, relinquished her phone and car keys to the boyfriend, and ordered him to keep them. She was afraid of leaving the house, finding drugs, and relapsing. Holed up, she endured withdrawal. "With the heroin and everything in there, it was gruesome."

"What made you so determined?"

"That fucking lady. Telling my boyfriend I was gonna relapse."

I laughed. "That woman did you a favor."

But Shauna didn't laugh.

So I stopped, too.

∽

Shauna peered over the deck's edge at my weedy yard. On the other side of the fence, a thicket of blackberry brambles tumbles into a wooded ravine. "What do you have? Dogs?"

"Chickens. We're down to three. Fox must have eaten the fourth."

"Foxes can be vicious."

---

[*]Vivitrol is an extended-release, injectable opioid antagonist, used for recovery from drug and alcohol dependence.

I glanced at my phone. It was nearly seven in the evening. I folded my knitting back into its bag. All that work, and still only an inch of hem finished. "Enough for one day? Maybe you could come back another time and tell me more? How you got — and stayed — sober?"

She nodded, staring at the chicken wire, seemingly lost in thought, then picked up her pack of cigarettes.

"You've been sober two years, you said?"

"Just about. That's something." She stood up, jangling her keys. "Yeah, I'll come back."

I rose, too, and leaned over the railing. The chickens sashayed around the edge of the barn, clucking, ready to roost for the night. "Hey, Cocoa," I called to the leader.

I glanced back at Shauna to introduce her to the chickens, but she was gone.

Gabriela ran out in her striped swimsuit. "Finally! I thought you were going to talk forever."

"She has quite a story."

"Can we still go swimming? I'm starving, too."

"Sure. I'll change quick. How about we pick up a pizza on the way?"

"Yes!"

six

The Thrush's Song

Over the next six weeks, I tried several times to arrange another time to meet Shauna, but my emails went unanswered. Finally, she responded, and we made a date to meet again on a Wednesday just after Labor Day.

September marks the end of summer in Vermont. While still warm, the autumn days are overlaid with a chill. Morning mist spreads through valleys. After reaching its lush peak, the garden begins to wither and die back. School starts. That year, Gabriela was a freshman in high school. Her first morning, I snapped a photo of her on our back deck before she headed off in new jeans, backpack slung over one shoulder, half smiling. In the background, our stony driveway curves down to the road, the mountains in the distance cupping that triangle of reservoir and beckoning an eager traveler. After she disappeared around the lilac hedge, I studied that picture on my phone. My youngest was already in her final childhood years.

The Friday before Labor Day, I stopped by the Hardwick Farmers' Market to ask Diane about the preholiday party she had attended the night before. She had sent me an email that morning, saying she had a story about the party that was too long and complicated for email. I bought dumplings and curried rice from the Nepali family, then stopped into her tent. Diane is the children's librarian at Hardwick's library, and her booth offers free books and crafts for kids. She had hired a high school student as a library aide for the summer. The teen was lying on the grass under the tent canopy, reading *Make Way for Ducklings* to twin girls, their dark, sweaty curls swirling over flushed foreheads. "Hey," I said to Diane. "What's the story about last night?"

She tipped her head. "Out here." We stepped just behind the circle of red and white pop-up canopies and sat with our backs to the circle of tents, our bare legs beneath summer skirts stretched out on the cool grass. "What'd you get?" she asked. "Dumplings?"

"You want one?"

"Well, they're your dinner . . ."

"I bought two orders."

"In that case, I'm starving." She dipped a plump dumpling into the container of spicy red pepper sauce I had tucked into the white box. "You should have brought me a napkin."

"I didn't realize I'd be feeding you. So? The party? I came for gossip."

"Well . . . I wore a nice dress. One I sewed."

"Naturally," I said.

"Lucian cleaned up, too. He put on a button-down shirt and washed his hands." During the two decades I'd known Diane, we'd often laughed about how, as a blacksmith, Lucian's hands were perpetually stained. "I was glad that he'd really scrubbed up, because, wow, was it a fancy party. We had dinner outside."

"Sounds nice. But what was too complicated for email?"

"Be patient. I'm getting there. Lucian drove home on Scott Road — you know, the back way. When we left, it wasn't even dark yet." The party was at a well-to-do farm a fifteen-minute drive from Diane and Lucian's house on dirt roads.

"Is there a plot to your story? He stops and picks up a snapping turtle as big as your kitchen table?"

"Not even close." Diane dipped another dumpling in the sauce. "Somehow I missed lunch today. The prep work for the market can be crazy." She bit into the dumpling, chewed, and swallowed. "Driving home, right by the old horse farm, we saw a woman walking along the road. She was only wearing a swimsuit, and it was starting to get cold. As we passed by, we saw she was crying. Lucian stopped, backed up, and rolled down his window. 'Do you need any help?' he asked. Well, turns out, she did."

"The plot thickens."

"She asked us to take her to the police station. Lucian said sure, and she got in the backseat. As he drove there, she told us that she and her boyfriend had been fighting while he was driving. The boyfriend pulled over and made her get out of the car, then drove off and disappeared. I was turned around, talking to her in the backseat, when I saw her slip something out of her swimsuit strap and put it in the bag she was carrying. *Sketchy*, I thought."

"Do you think she was high?"

"I don't know. At the station, Lucian parked, and I went in with her. The officer took us in the back and asked for a statement. She spoke so quietly I could hardly hear her. All I caught was that they'd been partying at Nichols Pond."

I nodded. Nichols, a pristine pond surrounded by forest and rocky cliffs to the north where peregrine falcons nest in the spring, had a reputation for raucous parties in its parking lot.

"She also said the boyfriend hit her. That's when the officer dialed AWARE* and gave me the phone. He said he'd step out and give us some privacy. I was thinking, *Hold on. All we did was stop along the road. I'm not 'with her' with her.*" Over the phone, the domestic violence hotline worker tried to get the woman to fill out a statement.

"What was her name?"

"Tammy."

"That's all? No last name?"

"That's all I got."

"Did she fill out the statement?"

"No. She said she'd done that before, and nothing happened."

"That's probably true. I've heard that before."

Meanwhile, the officer had called Tammy's friend who lives in the trailer park down the hill from my house. "When the friend appeared, she said, 'He did it again, didn't he? This has to stop.'"

"Ugh. What did Tammy say?"

"Nothing. She just stared at her feet. She was shivering in the station's air-conditioning, and I didn't have a sweater to give her."

---

*Aid to Women and Rape Emergencies.

Our friend Sarah walked by holding her three-year-old daughter's hand and slid a paper napkin into Diane's greasy fingers. "Looks like you need this. Aren't the dumplings fantastic?"

"The best."

In a hurry, Sarah called back, "We'll catch up soon!"

Painstakingly, Diane wiped each finger, from tip to knuckles to palm.

"Tammy went home with the friend?"

"Yes, but first we had her make a plan to call AWARE today and go in. By the time we left, a couple of hours had passed. When we got outside, Tammy hugged me and said I'd been her guardian angel. I was shocked. I didn't think of myself like that." She laid her crumpled napkin on the grass. "If it was just me in the car, I might have driven by. Lucian was the one who wanted to stop."

With the box of dumplings on the grass between us, I wrapped my arms around my knees. "You think she filled out those papers today?"

Diane shrugged. "Who knows."

From the market's center, a fiddle serenade drifted over the lush, damp grass toward the remaining abandoned granite shed along the field's far side. The roofline of the long, windowless shed sagged and rose unevenly, almost wearily, as if on the verge of collapsing.

"Lucian waited outside the whole time?"

"Yeah." She glanced over her shoulder at her adolescent helper who lay on her back, head propped up on her Birkenstocks, reading to the girls snuggled in her arms. "Here's the thing. That night, we lay in the dark, talking about those two parties that were just a few miles apart. We attended the swanky party." I nodded, thinking I could guess the guest list of the locally well-heeled. The hosts' children are students at Ivy League universities. I knew and liked these people; they were the same families who attended school board meetings and raised funds for libraries. "Just a few miles away, there's another party at Nichols, and this happens."

"Could have happened at the fancy party, too."

"Sure. But here's the thing: all night, while I was with Tammy, I kept thinking about how she could have been me. I left home at sixteen and lived in a school bus. How much of where I ended up was me, and how much was just circumstance?"

"That's a big question." I nestled the remaining two dumplings in that box in the second, full box. "It's funny, but when I bought these dumplings, I was remembering that I was a vendor at this market when Molly was an infant. That was our first year selling maple syrup. I was nursing her behind our table when a woman who was probably the age I am now came up and told me how glad she was to see me breastfeeding in public. She told me that, when she was a young mother, people told her to cover up when she nursed." We stood up, and I tossed the empty box in a trash barrel. "I was so young then. I didn't get how the time and place we live in matters. Like, if you're born into a family where one or both of your parents are doctors or attorneys, that's a logical path. Or if you're born into a family where martinis are served every night, drinking is what's normal."

"Or what if you're born into a family who keeps moving because there's no steady housing? Those things matter." Diane glanced at her tent, where a crowd of people had gathered. "I have to go."

✐

The next Wednesday, I took the afternoon off before meeting with Shauna, taking advantage of the lingering warm weather to repaint the lower clapboards on my house's northern side. Dressed in an old gray T-shirt and shorts, I spread drop cloths over flowerbeds bursting with hostas and lilies.

As I brushed glossy New England white over beat-up boards, worn and spotted with patches of remaining paint I had sanded smooth, I remembered how surprised I had been that Shauna recovered not by going to rehab but by confining herself to her house. In a way, Shauna's resolve reminded me of my own tipping point. I got sober pretty much how I became an alcoholic — as quietly as possible.

For years, I had wanted to get clean, too. I started and stopped, started and stopped, but I never had a serious reckoning with myself. Late one afternoon, when winter was again beginning to sink in its talons, I filled a glass of wine and took a long swallow. Gabriela, who was coloring at the kitchen table, went into the other room, where her sister was on the couch reading. I set a cutting board on the table and was about to dice a carrot and start making dinner. For a moment, I stood staring out the window at another snowfall beginning. That December, snow fell every single day — all thirty-one of those days — piling around our house like a barricade. I hated it.

From the other room, I heard Molly ask quietly, "Is she doing it again?"

Gabriela said, "Yes."

I finished the glass of wine, rinsed it out, then set the glass upside down in the dish strainer. I reached in a cabinet and pulled out a box of wine; by then, I was consuming so much wine that, for economy, I had switched from bottled wine to boxed wine. With a scissors, I cut open the cardboard box, pulled out the translucent bladder of wine, and jabbed the scissors' point into the bag. Like spilled blood, the wine rushed over my fingers and down the drain. I wasn't crying; I was utterly determined. I washed my hands and buried the empty bladder in the kitchen trash beneath the sink. Then I cut up the cardboard box and burned it in the woodstove.

I didn't reach out to AA, join a group, or attend counseling. I made no formal announcement to anyone. Instead, each morning, I silently repeated that my single goal for that day was not to drink. Every night, I sat on the couch and knitted, keeping my hands busy with yarn and needles rather than by lifting a glass. I avoided the corner store where I once regularly bought wine. As time passed, I took larger steps. I switched jobs. I left my marriage. Eventually, I woke up in the morning and thought about something other than not drinking. I never bought booze again.

But unlike Shauna, I kept my recovery a secret. I was afraid to admit that I had a problem, and once I decided to quit, I feared failing. Looking back, I can see the foolishness of that thinking. Even while drinking I had managed to do a fair amount with my life. But at the time, fear consumed me.

When I finished painting, I stood back, studying the clapboards, smoothing a few drips with my bristles. Just as I was folding up the drop cloths, Shauna arrived. "I don't know how I'm going to paint up there." I pointed to the peeling upper boards. "My ladder isn't tall enough. I'm not sure I'd even dare to climb that high."

Tipping her head back, Shauna appraised the roof's angle. "You need gutters. Otherwise, the water's always going to pour down that side."

I stepped back and assessed my house. She was right.

We walked around the house to the back porch. "Why don't we go inside? I tidied up yesterday, so the house is clean."

Shauna held up her pack of cigarettes. "Thanks, but I'm okay out here again. I'm going to smoke."

For the second time, I slid the saucer out from under the red geraniums and set it on the table. "I'll get some water. Make yourself comfortable."

In the kitchen, I stepped over Acer, who was rubbing against my ankles, hoping for an early dinner, and filled two glasses with water. On the deck, I set the glasses down and pulled up a chair. "How's work at the health center?"

"Busy. I deal with all kinds of crazy shit all day long. A lady called this morning and asked if she could see Dr. Buckley at eleven thirty. I'm like, probably fucking not, since he's booked out for months."

I laughed and resumed my knitting.

She continued, "I was sick, too. I missed some work. That's why it took me so long to get back to your emails."

"Sick? I'm sorry to hear that."

"I had a little slipup, actually."

"A slipup?"

"Yeah. But this time, I told my doctor after two weeks, not two years. That's progress, for me."

I held my needles still. "That's terrible. Let's just stop now. I'm so sorry."

She looked at me, her eyes thin ovals, quicksilver like minnows. "No, let's keep going. I just got complacent. I had almost two years. I thought, *I got this.*"

I spread the unfinished sweater over my knees. I had so much more to knit before I could wear it.

Shauna picked up her pack of cigarettes from the center of the table and moved it to the right side, then slid it to the left and shook her head. "You didn't make me do it."

"But . . ."

"No. If talking to you could help just one person, it's worth it."

"Are you absolutely sure?"

"Talking helps, really. That, and I'm on Vivitrol again."

Our eyes met for a moment. I thought how strange it was to learn so much about someone who knew nothing about me, apart from the fact that I needed gutters and didn't realize it.

"All right. But just say the word anytime you want to call this quits."

"Will do." Shauna pulled a cigarette from the gold American Spirit pack, flipped it around in her fingers, then lit it.

"So . . . what's this Vivitrol like?"

She exhaled a long stream of smoke. "Vivitrol's okay. It's a shot that lasts a month, unlike Suboxone, which I took every day. It kind of flattens out my life, so I'm just not excited about anything."

"That sounds like a rotten trade-off."

"Whatever." She shrugged. "The hard part is the emotional shit. I mean, I know what to do to get through sickness, but I don't know what to do to deal with feelings. After my brother died, I just didn't want to go there."

"Wait. That happened when you were nine?"

"I was nine when my first brother died."

"You had a second brother who died?" A cool wind swept across the deck, and I tugged my cardigan around my neck.

"Yeah. My younger brother. He was six when my first brother died. As a teenager, he got into a lot of drugs. One afternoon, he called me super upset, so I went to go find him. As I drove up, I saw all these lights. It was December, so I thought maybe they were for the holidays. But as I got close, I said to my friend sitting beside me, 'Those aren't fucking Christmas lights.' I pulled over and got out of the car. Someone came up to me and said he had just killed himself. He shot himself in front of his girlfriend."

Shauna wiped her eyes with a tissue. A breeze jangled the wind chimes hanging from the porch ceiling above her head. "It was awful. He was eighteen. I had to call my mom and tell her. After that, I was really serious about getting sober. I figured my mother shouldn't have to bury another kid."

"I'm so sorry."

The sparrows chittered in the slender-leaved box elders around the deck.

Shauna lit another cigarette. She breathed in.

∽

"Drugs," Shauna finally said after a long silence, tapping her cigarette on the ashtray. "Drugs are really good. That's the problem. When you're using, it's hard to imagine a life without them. For a long time, I didn't know how to deal with my feelings any other way. It's still hard for me to understand that getting high isn't an option anymore."

I nodded; I knew all too well how using could be a carapace, a place to tuck in and hide, where you could pretend your life wasn't unraveling.

"You can go weeks, months, even years without using, and then you smell something or hear a certain song on the radio, or you see

somebody, and — bam! — the cravings come right back. If you don't
keep your eye on that shit, it'll get you."

"It? You mean cravings for drugs? Or your past?"

"Both," she said emphatically. "I mean, fuck. Emotions don't go
away. If you bury them, everything comes crashing out when someone asks you for a fucking pen, and they get the last six months of
shit because they walked in at the wrong time."

I laughed. "So much shit can happen in six months."

She nodded, but she wasn't smiling.

I rubbed a fingertip around the edge of the saucer, staring at the
ashes sprinkled over its center. "What's it like for you to be sober?"

"It's harder. But it's better. My job is good, and I want to keep it. I
have money the day after I get paid. I've got my therapist and my
doctor on speed dial. I have Vivitrol. But I still crave drugs. I don't
talk to anyone who uses. It's easy for that shit to happen. You gotta
be on your game."

"At least to me, you seem impressively aware of your game."

With one hand, she waved away my words. "I have terrible days,
too. Just awful days. But if my mom can bury two kids and not have
a drug issue, I should be able to do it. When my brother killed
himself, his girlfriend was right there. She's now married and has
two kids. That's just freaking amazing. If she can stay clean, then I
should be able to stay sober, too."

"Can I reiterate my admiration again? So many people are just talk."

Shauna laughed. "Sometimes I downplay my trauma, but it made
me who I am. I change my own oil, take out the garbage. I run the
Weedwacker and stack firewood. I've repaired both mufflers on my
car, just because I could." Her jaw tightened. "But I don't want to be
taken advantage of." She told me how one night, she left her house
key in the outside lock. "When I woke up next morning and realized
what I had done, I was so relieved to have survived. I told myself, *See,
you're not going to fucking die.*"

"You're afraid here? In Hardwick?"

"I always lock up at night. Always have, always will." Cupping her hands around the lighter to shield the flame from the wind, she bent her head sideways and lit another cigarette.

"I lock up, too. I have a restraining order against my ex."

She tapped her lighter on the table. "So you know."

"I do. I get it."

⌖

As the dusk drifted in and the warm afternoon gave way to a crisp fall evening, our conversation wound down.

Shauna continued. "I still feel like I have a long way to go. But I feel lucky. I mean, in my addiction I never had sex for money or drugs. I never had to pick out of the Dumpster. My rock bottom wasn't as low as others. I'm thankful for that."

I thought of my own gratitude for how well things had worked out for me, despite my addiction; I had my daughters and house, my work, and my health.

Our cat Acer pushed his small pink nose against the window screen and meowed for his dinner. Gabriela usually fed him and his brother around this time.

"It's getting cold," Shauna said, zipping up her jacket.

"Just one more question. What advice would you give someone struggling with addiction?"

Shauna stared up at the porch ceiling painted the pale blue of forget-me-not blossoms, a New England tradition. She paused for so long that I was about to thank her and cut off our talk when she looked back at me.

"Recovery," she offered, "is possible. That's all."

"Oh . . ." I shivered. "It's warm in the house. Come in, please. I'll make tea."

She shook her head. "Thanks, but I should go. I've got to feed the dogs." She glanced at Acer sitting on the windowsill. "Looks like your cat is hungry, too."

"Thank you again."

We walked to the edge of the driveway. Then, after an awkward pause, we stepped forward and embraced. She was so much taller than me that I barely reached her shoulders.

When Shauna left, I gathered my two balls of yarn and went inside the kitchen. My girls hadn't returned, so I fed the cats, who rubbed against my ankles, mewling with hunger. From the refrigerator, I pulled out the red enamel pan of leftover lentil and carrot soup I'd made earlier that week and set it on the stove to warm.

Then I stepped out on the front steps to watch for my daughters. Last summer, I had painted these steps dandelion yellow, a hardware store deal for a can of paint mistakenly mixed. Standing there, my bare feet pressed together, I wrapped my cardigan around my torso. Shauna and I had much more in common than locking doors at night. Why had I revealed nothing?

⌁

I wandered into the garden and snapped a few cucumbers from the prickly vines. Finally, I saw my daughters running on the other side of the cemetery, racing each other home, ponytails bobbing. As they rushed up the path, I unlatched the garden gate and held up the cucumbers.

"Cukes. Yum. Did you put the soup on?" Molly asked, panting.

"Ten minutes ago." Together we walked up the steps. The girls untied their shoes on the back porch.

"We saw the bald eagles by the reservoir again," Gabriela said.

"What luck. I wonder if they're nesting there."

Molly opened the kitchen door, and the girls walked into our house. Before I headed in, too, I lined up my family's shoes beneath the overhang. Through the glass door, I saw Molly cradling Acer against her chest, his hind paws in Gabriela's hands as the two of them cooed over their beloved cat.

Hidden in the thicket behind our house, the hermit thrush — a

plain brown bird, small enough to fit in the palm of my hand —
trilled its rippling melody, those unseen pearls of sound.

In the center of the table where Shauna and I had sat that afternoon, the saucer was empty, save for crumbles of common garden
dirt and a scattering of ashes. When I wasn't looking, Shauna must
have gathered her crushed cigarette butts. I grasped the saucer to
dump the ashes and dirt over the railing then abruptly paused,
wondering: If I had lived Shauna's life, would I have had the strength
to get sober? And if I had, would I have risked that sobriety for a
stranger?

In the kitchen, my daughters joked with each other, setting the
table, the bowls and spoons clattering. The refrigerator opened and
closed; the faucet ran. I stood in the dusk, my breath stirring that
dusty ash.

seven

Night

That fall, I often walked alone in the long autumn twilight, the blackening sky shot through with streaks of crimson and purple. While I wandered along neighborhood streets where house lights were switching on, I thought of the morning I spent with Meg, listening to her story while I watched the sparkle of her diamond ring winding in and out of her brown hair. I kept thinking of what she and Shauna had overcome and the strange way John Baker's death connected our stories.

Late one afternoon, I was returning up our steep road when I heard coyotes howling. Pausing, I closed my eyes and listened. Before we married, Eric and I lived together in a trailer in rural Washington State while I was in graduate school and he worked as a house painter. One night, I ambled down the graveled driveway with a letter for the mailbox. Halfway down the driveway, I sensed a presence, then saw three coyotes standing in the nearby field, their shaggy outlines faintly visible in the starlight, eyes gleaming. I stepped backward, then whirled around, ran up the driveway and into the trailer, and slammed the door shut behind me, the envelope still clenched in my hand.

If I followed the footpath through those woods where the coyotes yipped their strangled cries, in twenty minutes I would reach Shauna's neighborhood. I wondered if she was returning home from work about now, listening as she stepped out of her car.

Suddenly, a horn blared. My eyes flew open, and I leaped to the side of the road. The UPS driver waved to me as she sped up the hill. I followed.

❧

The next morning, Halloween, dawned with a drizzle I expected to last all day. Earlier that week, Molly had flown to New Mexico to visit my parents. To liven up our quiet house, Gabriela invited friends home after school and made pizza for dinner. In the early evening, I walked around Hardwick with the girls — teens who considered themselves too old for costumes and trick-or-treating but didn't want to miss the festivities. When the misty rain fattened into a downpour, we sheltered inside the Hardwick Library, where Diane, dressed as Pippi Longstocking, distributed tiny Hershey bars to diminutive Harry Potters and Spider-Men. We lingered in the children's section, spookily lit for the holiday with candles and small lamps, then hurried home in a pounding rain.

All night, while the storm lashed our house, the cats and I lay awake, listening to the wind wailing. At first light, I zipped up my blue raincoat and wandered downtown. Running through the heart of the village, the Lamoille River roiled, frothy with dirt, tree branches, and junk — frayed plastic bags and lost shoes. Spellbound, I stood in the diner parking lot, staring over the cement embankment, the din of the early commuter traffic diminished by the pebble-filled water smashing against the retaining wall.

Rain fell steadily on my face as I walked home. In the kitchen, Gabriela was eating granola and maple yogurt at the table and said the superintendent had canceled school. Cooper Brook had flooded Route 14 near the Mountain View Snack Bar, and the highway was impassable. With the library closed, too, I worked at home. In the afternoon, the power went off. When my laptop battery drained, I pulled out a deck of cards from the kitchen drawer and found Gabriela in the dining room, busy with a protractor and her math notebook.

"Kid, want a break from geometry?"

"Hearts? I'll deal."

"Prepare to lose."

"You wish."

We played hand after hand, passing the Queen of Spades between us.

"When do you think the power will come back on?" Gabriela asked as the daylight ebbed.

"Today, sometime." I stood up and searched through a drawer in the hutch.

"What are you looking for?"

"Matches." I held up a crumpled box. From the upper cabinet, I took down a tarnished brass candlestick and a half-burned beeswax candle. Unable to use our stove without electricity, our dinner options were reduced to peanut butter sandwiches or cheddar cheese and crackers. "Let's go to Morrisville and get some dinner. The Wok N Roll?"

"You think Morrisville has power?"

"Maybe. Let's go see. I'm done working for the day."

Driving out of Hardwick along Route 15, we saw that the river had risen so high that its usual course was no longer visible. As in April's floods, the Lamoille appeared to have divided into two rivers — parting, merging, drifting apart again, but without the enormous ice floes of the spring breakup.

"Whoa . . ." Gabriela snapped photos on her iPhone.

Halfway there, traffic halted. Peering around the long line of red taillights, I saw that one lane of the highway had crumbled into the river. An emergency road crew swarmed the jagged ledge.

"Isn't that where they repaved this summer?" Gabriela asked.

"I think so." We inched forward, creeping by the snack shack, its windows boarded over with plywood for the winter. A flagger wearing iridescent yellow lifted a huge stop sign and halted me. In the valley behind him, violet dusk blurred the mountain ridgelines.

"Argh," I groaned, leaning on the steering wheel. "We nearly made it through." The wind hurled wet curls of dead leaves over the windshield.

"Are you in a rush?" Gabriela kidded me.

"Point taken. Like we're after the last moo shu pork in town."

Not far from our car hood, the flagger bent his head between his cupped hands, lit a cigarette, and inhaled. He turned away from us, shivering. A few minutes later, cigarette clenched in his teeth, he lowered the sign and motioned us forward. Passing him, I raised one hand.

"Really? You need to wave to everyone?"

"He's got a lousy job, and the evening's miserable."

As we rounded a hillside, we saw the swollen river in the valley below, water flowing around low-lying houses. Gabriela remarked, "Whoa. That doesn't look good . . ."

As we reached the outskirts of Morrisville, houses and streetlamps glowed, and we followed the lights into town. I pulled into the parking lot of the Wok N Roll, its red neon sign garish in the rain.

In the well-lit, white-walled restaurant, a crowd jostled around us. We waited in line, discussing the menu. House fried rice? Crab Rangoon? The woman who took our order said the wait was longer than usual. "Forty-five minutes."

"I guess we're not the only ones without power tonight."

She handed my change over the counter. "You got that right. Next!"

We stepped out of the crowded take-out joint and stood on the sidewalk. "No sense waiting around here," I said. "Let's go to Price Chopper."

We meandered down the supermarket aisles. In the baking section, I held up a box of lime Jell-O. "My grandmother served this. Maybe with canned fruit? I don't think I've made it even once."

"We ate it in elementary school. It's awful."

"I didn't know the schools fed kids that stuff." I set the Jell-O back on the shelf.

Farther down the aisle, I spied Ghirardelli white baking chocolate. "Brownies made from white chocolate? We need this."

"Definitely." She picked up two boxes.

We bought the chocolate and a jumbo pack of wintermint chewing gum. "Everyone likes it," Gabriela said, "when people bring in lots of gum to school." Back at the Wok N Roll, our order was waiting for us on the counter in a brown paper bag, stapled shut with my phone number scrawled in black marker across one side. In the drizzle, we drove out of town, the car redolent with gingery beef and green peppers. At that wrecked section of highway, the road crew was still working, their giant lamps powered by rumbling generators. After we passed through, the vehicles behind us turned off the road, one by one, disappearing into the unlit hills. Save for a sparse glimmer from the dash, the car's interior was dark. Our two meager headlights were the sole illumination I glimpsed in that wet night as we drove through the wide river valley.

That week, with her sister absent, Gabriela and I lingered over dinner and nightly Hearts games. At fourteen, she anticipated testing for her driver's permit next spring; the following year, she would likely score her license and her first steady job. Often those days as my youngest edged toward young adulthood, I found myself thinking about the year I first became a mother. "Did I ever tell you about the fall when Molly was a baby and just starting to crawl?" Even now, I remembered the heft of her wiggly body in my arms and how I loved to dress her in a pale pink sleeper my friend Sue Wagner had given her. "Your father was working out of state, and I was home alone with your sister."

"You never told me that. Where was he working?"

"In Connecticut. He had a job painting tennis courts with a man he had worked for that summer. They would drive south for two-week stretches, return for a weekend, and then head out Sunday night. Our house was just a camp with a few rooms then; we had plans, but we hadn't built any more. The woodstove was our only heat, and I ran out of firewood. Your uncle Nik came to visit, and I begged him to cut more with the chain saw."

Gabriela lowered the radio's volume slightly. "Was it hard to be alone with a baby?"

"It was much harder than I thought it would be. In those days, I was selling syrup at two farmers' markets — Hardwick's tiny one and the big Stowe market — and those were so much work. I'd leave your sister sleeping in her crib at night. Then I'd hurry down to the sugarhouse and clean up the sticky jars and jugs we had canned. I'd box up the syrup and get ready for the market."

"How would you know if Molly woke up and cried? You wouldn't have been able to hear her from the sugarhouse."

"I ran back to the house every few minutes or so." As I hurried along that narrow path through the woods, wielding a flashlight, I sometimes tripped on raised tree roots. "You remember how dark it gets around our old house? How you could hold your hand in front of your face and not be able to see it?"

"Yeah."

"And I was afraid of the dark in those days, too."

"Really?"

"I grew up in town, remember, not the country. But I forced myself to buck up. I knew I couldn't live there if I feared the dark."

We drove silently for a few miles, the headlights parting the darkness.

As we neared the turnoff for Hardwick, Gabriela said, "I never told you or Molly, but I was afraid that night." Staring straight ahead, her face was silhouetted by the dashboard light.

After a moment, I said as evenly as I could, "The night with your father?"

"Yes."

"When he was in the tree?"

"Yes. That night."

༄

Although Eric and I hadn't gotten along for years, we were together for more than two decades before I divorced him. In Hemingway's *The Sun Also Rises*, there's a famous line about how a character went bankrupt "gradually and then suddenly," which describes how our marriage fell apart. When I quit drinking, I expected sobriety to strengthen what lingered in our marriage. I took a job in a bookstore and stopped working with Eric in our sugaring business. We had disagreed for years, the business stuttering along, snarled in my guilt and his temper. Eventually, I realized I had mistaken the physical closeness of working together — boiling sap, canning syrup, attending farmers' markets — for intimacy.

Around that time, Eric joined a group protesting a wind tower project on a nearby ridgeline. During an argument over landownership, he and five others were arrested for trespassing. They lost in a jury trial, and he served a weekend in jail. After that, Eric had little regard for the law. Deciding that he didn't want to use money — he wanted to "drop out" of capitalism and go "off the grid" — he bartered carpentry work. Almost immediately, people took advantage of him and often failed to compensate him for his labor. He moved out of our house and started building a tiny cabin in a remote part of our hundred acres while living in a tent. A man named Timothy, whom Eric had once employed, reappeared. A zealous member of the anti-government sovereign citizens, Timothy had served time in federal prison for tax evasion, failure to pay child support, and threatening IRS employees. A national underground organization, the sovereign citizens numbers among its converts the infamous Oklahoma City bomber, Timothy McVeigh.

Within months, I filed divorce papers. Under the sway of Timothy, who insisted that the legal system didn't apply to sovereign citizens, Eric refused to appear in court. One morning, the town clerk in the southern Vermont town where we had married called me. Eric had phoned her and demanded that she erase his name from our marriage license. When she refused, he insisted that she was a public employee and was obligated to obey him. "Be careful," she cautioned me. "As town clerk, I've met plenty of drunk or crazy people. He stands out on the far end of scary."

Even more unnerving, Eric scrawled a handwritten letter to the county family court claiming that our daughters were his physical property and included black-and-white copies of the girls' photographs, identifying our daughters as exhibit A and B. My attorney mailed me a copy, although, apparently, Eric had done nothing illegal.

I stood at the mailbox, reading this letter over and over. I had taken that photo of Gabriela. She wore a floppy straw hat and was smiling so widely that I could see the gaps where her upper baby canine teeth had fallen out. I folded the papers and slid them back in the envelope, remembering how much Gabriela had cried as an infant; in the evenings, Eric would walk her around our grassy yard in his bare feet, massaging her back and singing sweetly to calm her. I would never understand what had happened to the man I had married.

In my divorce decree, the judge granted me full custody, title to the house, eight of our one hundred acres, and the sugaring equipment. By then, Eric and I were at a silent impasse. He lived in the woods on the ninety-two acres he owned; I lived with our daughters in the house we had built. He refused to pay child support, so I took a second job (ironically) writing for an upbeat parenting magazine.

In my years of living on that back road, the neighbors and I had often gone for walks, exchanged borrowed cups of sugar and bee balm clippings, or simply stopped by the mailbox to kvetch about the weather or muddy road. If Eric had been injured or sick — and not a muscular six-foot-three man who often shouted until the blue veins pulsed in his neck and forehead — friends would have split firewood and brought dinner, as they had so many years ago when he suffered a logging injury. But that summer, only one neighbor stopped in to ask if the girls or I needed help. Eric's unpredictable behavior and, likely, my wild and desperate unhappiness raised a barrier around our house that no one wanted to scale.

Shortly after we were divorced, I realized that I had to move. For months, Eric had been breaking in, leaving small signs of his presence — like the window screen removed from the bathroom — but never sufficient evidence to merit charges. I began to clear out years' worth of living, from business receipts to outgrown children's clothing. Desperate for cash, I listed the sugaring equipment for sale on Craigslist.

One afternoon when I was boiling spaghetti for dinner, Eric appeared in our yard. Seeing him, I walked out of the kitchen and stood on the porch. Angrily, he told me that he had been in the sugarhouse and noticed that I was cleaning the syrup pans. "Don't sell any of it. That equipment can't leave this property. I'm threatening you." A vein throbbed the length of his neck. He shook his fist at me and repeated, "I'm threatening you."

That evening, Eric returned on the tractor and dug a trench around the sugarhouse with the backhoe. "No one's going to carry anything out of here!"

When he refused to go after I asked him to leave, I told him I was calling the police.

"I don't care!" he shouted over his shoulder at me. He kept digging.

I went back to the house, took a deep breath, and dialed the state police. After I had waited about forty-five minutes at the top of the driveway, two cruisers appeared. By then, dusk had drifted in. Seeing their flashing lights, Eric ran into the woods. After talking with me, the three troopers followed him and returned an hour later, annoyed at their fruitless search. "This is a wild goose chase," the lead trooper informed me. "He's had his fun for the day, and I'm betting he's done for the night. There's an accident on the interstate where we're needed. We're leaving and won't be back here tonight to stumble around the woods in the dark."

The girls and I watched the cruisers drive away silently into the moonless night. Overhead, the Milky Way arched above our house, the stars a scattering of seed pearls in the summertime heavens. For a moment, I waivered. Several times that year, I had contemplated packing up my Toyota and driving away. But if I left, I knew that Eric would move back into the house and prevent me from selling the property. "Possession," he'd repeatedly told me, "is nine-tenths of the law." I needed that money to buy another house; without it, I guessed I would forever be struggling to pay rent, slipping further and further toward broke. I was goddamned if I'd walk away.

I told the girls, "Let's go in."

As we crossed the lawn, Eric called out, laughing, as if we were playing a game, "Good night, girls!"

Our daughters dashed through the kitchen door.

I shouted into the darkness, "Eric, stop scaring the children!"

In the kitchen we had built, where we had never bothered to install locks on doors or windows, my daughters and I stood huddled together, the lights off. Gabriela, eleven at the time, whispered, "I don't think I can live in this house anymore."

Her words shamed me. What had we done to this child?

Molly pleaded, "You have to lock the basement door."

To lock the door — something we rarely did, as there had never been any need — I had to walk around the house in the dark and snap the padlock closed. I had always pictured our two-and-a-half-story cedar-shingled house as a tall, narrow ark, sheltering our family against Vermont's long winters, but that night I saw ourselves as shipwrecked, marooned on an island surrounded by a vast sea. At the back door, I snapped that padlock closed — futilely, he and I both knew — to keep him out.

∽

The following day, Eric called Molly and told her he had hidden for hours in the maple tree just outside Gabriela's bedroom window. He gloated as if he had discovered a clever hiding spot in a children's game. He must have watched me walk beneath the branch where he was perched.

That evening, Eric plowed under my garden with his tractor, and I phoned the state police again. When I told the trooper about Eric sitting in the tree, he said, "In the tree? You're kidding me."

There was no kidding about any of this.

Years later, while seeking an extension of a restraining order, a state's attorney asked me why I hadn't left the state and started over. I fumbled an explanation that I didn't want to uproot our daughters. What I should have told him is that I no longer lived in a world where the rules I once believed in applied. If he wanted, Eric could track me down wherever I went. Since he no longer lived in the rational world, by extension, neither did I.

⌒♯⌒

I touched Gabriela's knee. "I was afraid that night, too."

She shifted and knocked my hand off. "Why'd you stay with him for so long? You should have just left."

"It wasn't that simple." The electricity was still out as we drove into the village. A scattering of house windows glimmered with smudges of light from candles or camping lanterns. "How can I explain? That fall I told you about, when your father returned from working in Connecticut, we had a fight that lasted three days. He didn't want to work that winter; he wanted to take time off and wander around in the woods. But if he didn't work, we couldn't pay the mortgage. Molly was so young, still nursing and barely crawling. I kept asking him, 'But how are we going to get by? We have a child now. We're a family.'"

I turned at the T in the center of the unlit downtown. Although the evening was still early, the road was empty of traffic. No one was walking their dogs across lawns or on sidewalks. "One night, I ran out of the house and drove away with Molly. We ended up in Montpelier. I walked all over town with her in a backpack. Finally, I stopped on Main Street in front of this fancy inn. I wanted to go in and rent a room. I was just so darn tired. I imagined letting her crawl on the carpet while I lay on a bed. I stood there for what seemed like hours, Molly's little fingers tugging at my braid. And then I got back in the car."

"But why? Why didn't you leave?"

"I've thought so much about this. Maybe if I had family nearby I would have had somewhere to go. In those days, I hadn't even met friends with babies. I guess I didn't see any way out."

I pulled into our driveway and slipped the key from the ignition.

She opened her door, triggering on the dome light over our heads. We blinked in the sudden brightness. "Wait," I said. "Maybe the truth is, I didn't want to break up our family. I wasn't ready to give up." Gabriela stared down at her lap. For a moment, I remembered this teen as a little girl. Even as a toddler, she was resolute — not stubborn, but simply steady. Watching her, for the first time I wondered if that night's box of darkness might have fed the seeds of her courage. Was it possible, I wondered, that fear wasn't only a curse but a fortuitous strength, too?

"I want you to know, Gabriela, I've never regretted going back that night. I regret plenty, especially the drinking and how weak it made me, but I got you, and I wouldn't have gotten you if I'd left then."

"You could have been happier."

"Without you? Never, daughter. I was meant to be your mother. Everything else in my life may not amount to scratch. But you and Molly? You're my everything."

We got out of the car and stood for a moment, listening to the nearby river roaring steadily as it rushed over rock and sand. A balmy wind gently stirred the ends of my long hair. Overhead, storm clouds scudded across the sky, and the moon abruptly burst into view, a nearly full orb, drenching us with its ethereal radiance.

"Awesome!" Gabriela exclaimed, her arms wrapped around our paper bag of dinner.

Before us, our white house shimmered in the night, with its five regular-sized windows and the smaller one in my office, like an eye winking in the moonlight, welcoming us. Then the clouds veiled the moon again, draping us in darkness. By the light of my cell phone, we walked up the wide steps and went in.

I struck a match and lit the candle. As I unwound my scarf, my finger found a hole. The end must have snagged when I wasn't paying attention, maybe caught by a twig as I walked through the forest. Gabriela unfolded the lids of the white paper boxes, releasing the spicy scent of ginger. I set two bowls on the table, and we sat down. Gabriela pinched a peapod between her chopsticks and held it over a coil of lo mein. "These are my favorite things to eat in the garden."

"Standing barefoot and picking them from the vine?"

"Exactly."

When we finished eating, she held her fortune near the flame and read it aloud. "Your shoes will make you happy today."

"Maybe that should say 'your boots' on a soggy night like this. Open the other cookie and read mine, will you? This light's too dim for me to read without my glasses."

She ripped the cellophane bag, cracked the cookie, and squinted at the white paper fortune in the dim light. Then she looked at me and laughed.

"What?"

"You'll never guess," she said, giggling.

"Come on," I said. "How bad is it?"

"It's blank." She handed me the tiny slip.

I turned the paper around and around, then busted out laughing, too. "Some kind of cosmic joke, maybe."

"Maybe. Or maybe that's just your fortune. Write it how you want it." She pushed a pen across the table to me.

MIND

eight

A Willing Heart

By Monday morning, the river had receded back into its banks. After Gabriela walked to school, I emailed Katie Whitaker, a registered nurse at the Hardwick Health Center whom Jeri Wohlberg had suggested I contact, and asked if I could buy her lunch. Ever since I had attended that Narcan training, I'd been thinking about the relationship between genes and addiction, remembering that presenter who described addiction as a genetic disease that requires medical treatment like any other disease. The idea was at odds with my understanding of addiction as a bad habit, a personal weakness that I overcame by willpower alone, and I wanted to learn more. Katie quickly responded to my brief query and said she would be happy to meet and talk about the center's recovery program. She suggested eleven thirty at the Hardwick Village Restaurant to beat the noon rush.

The Hardwick Village Restaurant, a breakfast-lunch-and-dinner joint known around town as "the diner," is located at Hardwick's central, three-way intersection, often clogged with school buses, milk or log trucks, and commuter traffic. On that raw November midday, I walked downtown from our house, arriving before Katie and scoring us a window booth. I had just ordered coffee when she appeared at the door in pink-and-yellow-flowered scrubs. Ringed by long golden curls, her face glowed with a lingering summer tan. We made eye contact, and I waved her to our booth.

She slid onto the bench opposite me. "I'm Katie." She smiled kindly.

"I'm Brett. Thank you so much for meeting me."

"I love that, as a librarian, you're asking these questions. I'm passionate about my patients and helping people understand them better."

I peeled off the top from a plastic container of creamer and dumped it into my coffee. "I attended a Narcan training through the

Department of Libraries. That presentation gave me some insight, and now I'm looking for more information."

A woman in jeans with a silver braid pinned into a bun handed us laminated menus. "Specials are chicken potpie, Cobb salad with local Jasper Hill blue cheese — very delicious — and lamb meatballs. I'll be back shortly for your order." She dashed away.

The diner's tables and booths were beginning to fill with a chattering crowd.

Without opening her menu, Katie said, "I'm a big fan of the Caesar salad here. With extra lemon."

"That sounds like a good choice."

The waitress returned with two glasses of ice water, and we both ordered salads. When she gathered our menus and left, I said, "Thanks again for taking time out from your day. My mother was a nurse, although she's retired now. Her work was incredibly challenging at times, although, generally, I think she loved it."

"So you know, then, how this can be an all-consuming occupation. What kind of nursing did your mother do?"

"When I was a kid, she floated around different floors, from pediatrics to postoperative. She worked nights, and often told us fascinating stories at breakfast about what had happened while we were sleeping. I vaguely remember some story about an ER doctor who had a crack-up."

"Years on the night shift? That's tough."

"In retrospect, I realize that my mother must have been sleep-deprived for much of my childhood."

Katie laughed. "I'm sure she was."

"When I was in college, she took a day job on the hospital's locked psych ward. She loved that work. Actually, I think she liked everything but the cancer ward — and the administration, I suppose."

"I think many nurses share your mother's feelings about hospital bureaucracy. Sometimes, of course, it's just luck of the draw about where you're working."

"Have you always worked with people in recovery?"

"Oh, no. I began as a labor and delivery nurse at the hospital in Morrisville. In that position, I worked with many mothers, and that experience opened my eyes to how prolific the opioid problem is in this part of the state."

"Just for my own time line, when was that, approximately?"

She took a sip of water and set her glass down. "Around 2011. I was seeing a lot of expecting and new mothers who were using and looking for help to quit. At that time, women who needed treatment had to travel to Burlington, often an hour or more away. I helped start the Close to Home program, which has a mission to treat women in their communities, if at all possible."

"How successful was that approach?"

"Very. The program is still operating. One of my biggest takeaways is that accessibility to treatment is essential for a good outcome. I also witnessed that offering treatment without judgment or disparagement is far more likely to be effective. During the development process, I got very interested in addiction treatment and switched to working in the MAT program."

"MAT? Wait. You're losing me here."

"MAT is medication-assisted treatment. The short explanation is it's an evidence-based program that uses medications, such as methadone or buprenorphine, to help people physically wean themselves off substances. At the same time, participants are helped to stabilize other areas of their lives. Maybe they need secure housing or employment, or simply a chance to breathe, to increase their chances of a successful recovery. Many people testify that the program is incredibly effective."

"Just so I'm clear, MAT considers addiction a disease and not simply bad behavior?"

"Addiction is a disease. I'm frequently asked this question. When I run into resistance, I always suggest that people widen their understanding of disease. Look —" Katie raised her glass again and then set it down without drinking "— human beings are complex, and our diseases are often complex, too. Whereas a common cold is pretty simple — someone who catches it is miserable for a few days and then recovers — something like heart disease is far more complicated. Some people have a genetic predisposition to heart disease, but many other factors contribute to heart disease, too, such as diet and exercise, smoking and stress. To genuinely help that person get healthier, we need to address not just their physical ailments, like high cholesterol, but also their life's circumstances. So it goes with addiction. Does that make sense?"

"I suppose. Until recently, I hadn't thought of addiction as a disease; I always considered it more of a habit that needed to be broken. I know the causes of addiction are often invisible. Still, it still seems to me that addiction is different in some kind of way from heart disease."

"It is." She tucked her long curls behind her ears. "One way to think of addiction is it's a disease with both a physical and a social-emotional component. Opioids are phenomenally physically addictive. When someone begins ingesting opioids regularly — for whatever reason, whether they had a legal prescription or experimented at a party — their body chemistry adjusts and they begin to crave more and more narcotics, creating a physical habit. But when you're on that path of opioid abuse, often you're trying to soothe something deeper. Narcotics obscure pain; that's their function. And if you can treat your pain with drugs, whether it's a physical or emotional wound, why wouldn't you?"

"So what's the magic of MAT?"

The server, hurrying by, dropped two bundles of silverware wrapped in paper napkins on our table.

Katie unrolled hers and smoothed the napkin over her lap. "It's not magic. That's a misunderstanding. Narcotics are incredibly powerful substances that co-opt the body's chemistry. MAT tapers the body off those narcotics. At the same time, we offer wraparound services like job training, tailored to each patient, and counseling is always part of this process. In the wider view, MAT is a piece of Vermont's harm reduction approach."

"I'm lost again. I'm not familiar with harm reduction."

"Okay . . . How can I best explain this? Think of harm reduction as a willingness to meet people where they're at, but not in a punitive way. The goal is to minimize immediate danger, or harm, and buy time until people are willing to accept treatment. Recently, fentanyl* showed up on the scene and completely changed the game. The risk of overdose escalated tremendously. The question rapidly became, 'How do we keep people alive until we get them into treatment?' Now we give away fentanyl testing kits, clean needles, and Narcan, while always offering options for long-term recovery. Harm reduction means that we should do everything we can to keep you alive today, even if you're not willing to accept treatment, because tomorrow might be the day you start on the path to recovery. No matter how badly you think you've messed up your life — maybe your family is estranged, or you're jobless and homeless — your life is always worth saving."

I unwrapped my silverware and straightened the knife and fork on my napkin. "What do you say to people who criticize MAT for perpetuating addiction or swapping one drug for another?"

"That resistance to MAT is a kind of Not In My Backyard mindset. It's really difficult to overcome, and its root is the stigma surrounding opioid abuse. But are we supposed to not offer treatment to people who desperately need it? No one would withhold medication from someone who suffers from heart disease, even if their own behavior has been a contributing factor to the progression of that disease and they still aren't eating well or exercising."

The waitress reappeared and slid our salads on the table. A strand of silvery hair had unraveled from her bun, and she tossed her head. "Anything else right now?"

Katie asked politely, "Could I please have a few extra lemon slices?"

"Of course." She hurried away to her next table.

With her knife and fork, Katie cut her large lettuce leaves into pieces.

---

* A synthetic opioid, fentanyl is fifty to one hundred times more potent than heroin.

Through the window, I noticed gray clouds, carrying rain or maybe early snow, descending on the town. A white husky, its fur matted with mud, wandered along the riverbank below the diner. I wondered if the dog was lost, or merely not sure where it was headed — a creature not so different from myself. I pressed my fork tines into a crouton. "Are you suggesting I should consider addiction a social disease, too?"

"Exactly. Look, nobody decides to pursue a life of substance abuse." Katie sprinkled pepper over her salad. "If we're really going to understand addiction with some fidelity, we have to move beyond that stigma attached to substance abuse. We have to quit pointing fingers."

The waitress rushed by with a plate of french fries in one hand and set a saucer of lemon slices on the table. "Love that lemon." Katie squeezed a slice over her salad and laid the yellow rind on the edge of her plate. "Addiction is a disease that runs in families. I've worked with hundreds of people over the years, and I've seen how nearly impossible it is for people to change their environment. Say you make it to recovery. Your family, your friends, your buddies, they all come looking for you. You're one of them, and why have you left? Your drug dealer also seeks you out: You're a valuable commodity, and if you quit using, others might quit, too. You're bucking an economy by going cold turkey. Often during that initial treatment phase, people become isolated and lonely, which contributes to relapse. Look, I don't want you to leave with the impression that harm reduction is touchy-feely. It doesn't mean you should go and do whatever you want. If you're in the throes of a serious addiction and you mess up, you can die. Don't mistake compassion for gooiness. But healing requires compassion."

"You really believe compassion is essential?"

"I don't just believe it. I know it. Many of my patients have been treated horribly in their lives, and that includes a medical profession that stigmatizes them. Harm reduction, instead, acknowledges, yes, this is where you are, in a way that isn't punitive but compassionate.

This approach provides resources and support, so people can get on stable enough footing to begin to help themselves. More than anything, though, harm reduction offers a viable path out of addiction when it appears there's no hope."

I held my fork with a crouton over my plate. "What you're saying reminds me of a line from Marx: 'Men make their own history, but they do not make it as they please; they do not make it under self-selected circumstances, but under circumstances existing already, given and transmitted from the past.' Last January, a man who lived near my library died. He had a drug problem, and I keep wondering: How much of his problem was created by difficult circumstances in his life, and how much was his own doing? I know it's an impossible question. Still, I can't help but wonder." On the muddy bank, that bedraggled dog prodded its snout into the earth, determined to unearth treasure. "None of us want to believe we live in circumstances we don't choose, right? We want to believe we're steering our own fate."

"That belief is natural. But do my work, and you'll soon see that circumstances matter greatly."

"The thing is," I said, "I keep thinking about that man, but of course I'm thinking about myself, too. I don't have any answers, but I'm beginning to see that, even as strangers, we're more connected to one another through circumstances than I realized. And that may not necessarily always be bad."

"I guess circumstances made us have lunch together, right?" Katie dug her fork into her lettuce. "I love this kind of salad, such a great combination of fresh greens and crunchy croutons."

For a few moments, we ate in silence, then Katie said, "In my job, I see many terrible things. I've had hundreds of patients who live in circumstances they never would have chosen. But I also witness people who do put the pieces of their life together again after unimaginably bleak experiences, like relapsing and almost dying." She set her fork and her knife across her empty plate. "What I do is really powerful work, but it goes to the very darkest places and can be draining. I love it, but for people who get burned out, I think, *Go be a florist. Go find some joy in life.*"

I laid my fork down, too. "But you do find joy in your work. I hear that in your voice. I can see it in your whole body."

Katie smiled. "Absolutely."

The waitress stopped by and stacked our plates. "Anything more, ladies?"

"I'll take the check," I told her, "whenever you have time." The waitress nodded, then hurried away.

"Thank you for the delicious salad — but before I lose this train of thought, I want to say that, as a society, we don't punish people for getting cancer, a disease we don't know nearly enough about. Likewise, the science behind addiction isn't fully known. More research is needed. Our bodies act and react in ways that we often don't understand."

Samara Oblonsky, who had volunteered at my library's pie breakfast last winter, walked over to our table and said hello. Katie told me that she and Samara, who is also a nurse, worked together a few years ago. As they spoke, I glanced out the window across the river, looking for that dog, but he had disappeared.

"Look me up when you need more volunteers," Samara told me, then returned to her table.

"It's so nice to run into people you haven't seen for a while. I'll have to call her and catch up." Katie glanced at the time on her phone.

"I know you have to go back to work, but do you have time for one more question?"

"Of course."

"We've talked about individuals and addiction, but what's the larger context? When I think about your heart disease analogy, I see a society that encourages ill health: eating processed food, not exercising enough, drinking alcohol. Does our society foster addiction, too?"

"That's a huge question. Maybe it's *the* question." She set her empty water glass at the edge of the table for the server to collect.

"We've talked about how Vermont is doing a good job of putting out the immediate fire, but what starts that fire? Hello? That's a sociopolitical landscape that needs to be dealt with."

"You mean poverty in this area?"

"What I mean is, we're one of the richest countries, yet our outcomes are so poor. You can't look at this epidemic in a vacuum. Young people growing up in this area, who one generation ago were dairy farmers or loggers, today have few decent job prospects and educational opportunities. We know opioid abuse is pervasive across all socioeconomic levels. But the odds are stacked against people who don't have resources, and entrenched poverty does nothing to deter the proliferation of heroin."

"I get that. The thing is . . . people live their lives in the here and now, so what's the immediate way forward to helping people?"

"My answer to this huge question? On a grand scale, we need an economy that supports everyone. On a more personal level, maybe this looks like a compassionate person with a heart willing not to judge you and who can offer resources you're willing to accept. I see people come into the ER after an overdose, with charges racked up, and their kids lost to state custody, and their path forward seems impossible. Some people don't ever get out of addiction. But the whole point of harm reduction is that, while you're alive, it's never too late, no matter how hopeless your life may appear."

Around us, silverware clattered, the lunch crowd buzzing merrily.

"This is such a strange time," I said. "My daughter is studying the fall of Rome in world history. Talking with her made me wonder if we're living through the crumbling of the mighty American empire."

"The world can feel that way, but I don't want to go down that rathole of despair." Katie took a deep breath and tossed her long curls. "When I talk about these issues, I always try to end on a positive note. I keep reminding myself we're lucky to live in the Shire of Vermont, as imperfect as this shire might be."

The waitress whisked by us, arms raised, her hands full of small plates of cream pie slices, each crowned with a cherry.

Katie sighed. "Hopefully, as a society, we can start to look at ourselves more honestly and begin to uproot what's poisoning us. Either that, or I'll move to Canada or Sweden or somewhere else."

⁑

Rummaging in my backpack for my wallet, I pulled out my knitting and settled it beside my crumpled napkin.

"What are you making?" Katie asked.

"A sweater. Here's one sleeve." I smoothed flat the yellow-flowered cuff.

"You've done beautiful work."

"The pattern is insanely complicated, or maybe it's just I'm slow-witted. I've redone it a zillion times."

"The finished sweater will be worth it. Thanks again for lunch."

We stood and hugged. Then Katie hurried through the door.

I left the check folded around bills beneath my coffee cup, pulled on my jacket, and walked home in the cold drizzle.

When I left that morning, Molly was mixing dough for cinnamon rolls and listening to Stephen Colbert, and I longed to be in our warm, lemon-yellow kitchen, sweetly fragrant with the yeasty scent of rising dough. I cut through the cemetery. Down the hillside, I spied the row of mobile homes on the upper tier of the trailer park. As I hurried through the sleet, I remembered the winter Molly progressed from crawling to walking. Strapped for income, I took a temporary job working for the 2000 census, collecting data in nearby hardscrabble North Wolcott. On one stop along a dirt road, an older woman invited me in from the cold. Her mobile home was situated on a ridge, the snow wind-sculpted so high around the trailer that not much of the rust-streaked metal was visible. Clutching my census clipboard, I followed her down a hall reeking of ripe garbage. Our trainer had warned us about folks who would view a government employee and a checklist of questions with skepticism and sometimes outright hostility. What I hadn't expected to find were lonely people, hungry for company at the tail end of bitter winter. In the kitchen, her husband sat in a wheelchair beside a window with a view of a snow-covered field and the distant mountains.

On the kitchen table was a paper plate printed with green holly and bright red berries. Her hands trembling a little, the woman painstakingly removed Saran wrap from the plate. Beneath it lay half a dozen white star cookies, sprinkled with pink and purple sugar crystals. The woman urged me to try one. She offered to put on the kettle and make tea. Politely, I refused both. I was there on business, with a stack of forms and dozens of stops to finish before I headed home. I couldn't afford to linger.

Now, through the bare branches of trees, I saw the red tin of our barn roof. Where the footpath wound through the hydrangeas and joined our lawn, I paused, my soaked jacket clinging to my shoulders and body. Nearly two decades and a lot of living later, my refusal of that cookie and cup of tea shamed me. Standing in what promised to be an all-day, maybe days-long frigid rain, I knew Katie would have relished the cookie.

nine

The Zombie Apocalypse

On a drizzly Wednesday morning a few weeks later that fall, I was reading in the dentist's office, waiting to have a tooth checked, when Molly texted me and asked if I'd heard what happened in Woodbury.

— No idea.

— Two houses burned down. Fire department found two bodies.

— Terrible!

— Two dogs were shot. Looks bad. Maybe a drug deal gone wrong.

— What? Where?

An assistant in red scrubs opened the waiting room door and called, "Brett?"

I glanced at my phone and saw Molly had typed, "Bliss Road," before slipping it back in my bag and following the assistant into the exam room.

While she stood reading my chart, I sat in the dentist's chair and stared out the window at a picnic table strewn with a scattering of wet maple leaves.

"Any new medications? Or changes in health?"

"No."

"I'll have to x-ray your tooth." She propped my chart in a plastic holder. "You work in Woodbury?"

"I'm the librarian."

"I heard about what happened last night in your town." She fiddled with an X-ray machine in the corner.

"What'd you hear?"

"What everyone else did, I'm sure. The fire department discovered two bodies in South Woodbury. Open wide, please." She slid the X-ray insert into my mouth and adjusted it. "Some sketchy stuff must be happening there. Don't move."

She walked out of the room and clicked the camera.

Down the hallway, I heard Dr. Allen laugh. "It's so windy I just about blew off my bike riding in."

"What sane person is biking now?" his assistant asked. "Summer's flown the coop."

Dr. Allen entered the room and washed his hands. "Good morning, Brett. Wild weather out there."

His assistant inserted my X-ray into the illuminated box. Dr. Allen pointed to a black smear at the base of a tooth in my lower front jaw, then looked at me. "Remember how we talked about root canals failing? And infection setting in again?"

"I know the infection's back. I can feel it."

Fifteen minutes later, I left with a referral for an oral surgeon and instructions to call for an appointment that very day. Although I had intermittently noticed a gnawing pressure in my jaw, particularly on damp days, the news dismayed me. Even after anteing up for expensive dental work, I would be a woman with a missing front tooth. I had been warned that this tooth, once infection set in, would not be long for this world.

Running late to open the library, I had forgotten that Chrissy had volunteered to reorganize the children's jumbled nonfiction shelves. I was gathering large-print John Grisham novels for a patron's grandfather when she showed up, wearing a green sweatshirt with a vanilla ice cream cone silkscreened on the back, advertising DELL'S SWEET SHOPPE.

"You heard, of course?" she asked.

"Seems like everyone has."

Chrissy started in the dictionary section, pulling out books and reshelving. "Whoa, this is quite a mess. Glad I'm here. I heard the fire department was called out in the middle of the night for a structure fire. When they got there, they found two houses blazing. The fire burned so hot that something in the house started going off — probably guns or ammunition. It must have been mayhem. How scary is that? For a volunteer fire department?"

I chose another Grisham and set the books on my desk.

Even though only two of us were in the library, Chrissy lowered her voice. "You heard they discovered two bodies?"

"Who were they?"

"A man and a woman — not married, I don't think. I forget their names. They're not part of my, ah, circle. But I heard Viola Fusilli had hired the woman as a housekeeper and babysitter. She had to let her go earlier this year. The woman wasn't showing up when she was supposed to. Viola thought she was doing drugs. But can you imagine? A volunteer fire department having to find that?" Chrissy stepped back from the shelf, both hands clutching books by their spines. "You know what brought this in."

"Shh," I whispered, tipping my head toward the window. "The kindergartners are coming."

Chrissy bent down to a lower shelf, a tiny silver cross around her neck swinging over her sweatshirt collar. "This is drug business, in our town."

I opened the door and stepped out to meet the kids, their cheeks satiny red from running in the rain.

"Hurray!" James Stratton called out. "Stories!"

∽

At dinner that evening, Molly asked if I'd heard any more details about the fire.

"Nothing new. The names haven't been released yet."

"See why I'm afraid when you invite drug users — even former ones — into our house?"

"Molly, this isn't the same."

She lifted the white enamel bowl of sautéed kale and asked, "Either of you want the rest of this?"

"Nope." Gabriela carried her water glass into the kitchen to refill it.

"Take it," I said.

Molly dumped the greens on her plate. "You can see why I don't like what you're doing."

"Sure, but still —" I glanced at Gabriela as she sat down again. "I'm not going to argue. Let's not go down that rathole."

"Agreed."

But the subject lay between us. We didn't joke while brushing our teeth that night. When my daughters went to their rooms, the house was quiet, and I laid in bed, worrying. Crime? Homicide? Of course I feared these things. And yet I didn't regret in the least that I had invited Shauna to our house.

∽

The next afternoon, a retired teacher named Galvin Wilson visited the library and asked to use a laptop, as his connection was down. A tall man with a waist-length pointy white beard and who always wore cowboy boots, Galvin was looking for news about the fire and wondered what I had heard. "What the heck is happening in our town?" he asked me. "I live up the road from that scene."

I covered the big table with old newspapers. The third and fourth graders would be arriving shortly to do an art project. "I don't know that part of Woodbury very well."

"Well, I'll tell you, there's something terribly wrong with my neighborhood." He sat down in a wing chair with a laptop, muttering to himself. "Jesus, they didn't even spare the dogs."

I dropped a stack of used magazines on the table. All morning, I had been imagining that midnight scene: crackling fire, choking smoke, guns discharging in the inferno, and the firefighters' confusion.

Galvin closed the laptop and leaned back in the chair. "Here's what disturbs me, Brett — no one is saying anything. That's not like the small-town Vermont I know, where people run their mouths. If the media shows up, people usually talk. But this?" He shook his head. "Everyone says, 'No comment.' No one saw anything. People are scared."

I scattered scissors and glue sticks around the table. "I understand that fear. Homicide rarely happens around here. When it does, it's almost always connected to domestic abuse."

He stood up and returned the laptop to my desk. "Here's the thing. There's homicide, and there's homicide. With all that ammunition, I doubt this was a lovers' imbroglio. Which begs the question: How did that happen in our little town? Except for Route 14, we don't even have a paved road."

"Maybe it was random?"

"Bullshit. I don't mean to be alarmist, but the people behind this are bad, bad news."

"I have a class coming in any minute now."

"I'm just saying, we all need to be careful."

Maya ran through the door with her haiku in one hand. "Miss Brett!" She hugged me.

"Hey, there, Archer," Galvin said to one boy. "How's your education going?"

"They're making us write poetry."

Galvin laughed. "You're going to knock up against worse things in this world than poetry, son." He rubbed the top of the boy's head and left.

For an hour, the children slashed into magazines with scissors and shared their three-line poems with me. I wrote the class favorite on the library's chalkboard:

> Mud — *squishy, squashy*
> *My bare toes squeeze wet black dirt*
> *Mom yells, Wipe your feet!*

When they left, I swept the paper scraps into the recycling bin. Galvin and Chrissy were right; something nefarious had happened in this town. I was afraid, too. What rational person wouldn't be? But as I wiped glue streaks from the table, I cautioned myself against letting fear blind me this time.

✑

At soccer playoffs later that week, I ran into Aaron Cochran, the Hardwick chief of police, sitting in a lawn chair on the sidelines and watching his daughter, who played for the same high school team as Gabriela. I stopped and said hello, then asked, "About this Woodbury news? I know you're not on duty now, but would you mind if I stop by your office sometime? I know you don't have answers you can share about that case, but I have some questions about substance abuse and law enforcement more generally."

"Sure. Woodbury's not my jurisdiction, but I'll always talk about public safety."

"Should I send you an email?"

The crowd roared as our kids' team scored a goal.

"Email's good. We'll set up a date."

At home that evening, while the girls did their stretching exercises, I emailed Cochran. He replied quickly, and we agreed to meet the next morning.

Located on the hill between the town offices and the high school, the Hardwick Police Department occupies the former Hardwick Health Center, where I used to bring my girls for well-baby checkups. Waiting in the small lobby, I listened to the dispatcher behind glass who was speaking calmly on the phone. "Excessive speed, you say? Any idea about the vehicle? Maybe the plate or who was driving?"

Cochran opened the locked door and invited me in. The chief is about my age, has two daughters, and lives not far from my house. Around town, he has a reputation for passionately pursuing law enforcement. "Good morning on this gloomy fall day. Great game yesterday." He led me to a room in the back, where we sat with the door open. "What is it you're looking for?"

"I think you know I'm the Woodbury librarian?"

"Of course."

"I'm sure you remember the death last January that was connected to my library."

"I do."

"So after that suicide, I felt compelled to learn more about opioid abuse. I've reached out to medical professionals and people in recovery. One thing I learned, which honestly surprised me, is that addiction doesn't happen in a vacuum; it affects so many other people. But the Woodbury homicides made me realize that fear and crime are an enormous piece of understanding addiction in our society, too. Those questions brought me to you." I crossed my legs. "I grew up in New Hampshire, and these kinds of drugs didn't really seem to be around when I was in high school."

Cochran leaned back in his chair. "I grew up around here, in Walden, just over the Hardwick town line. I don't remember seeing anything like this back then, either. Years ago, marijuana was a big deal, but now we're talking about heroin."

"Help me understand the scope of this, will you? Until recently, I wasn't even aware it was an issue around here."

"Oh, opioids are a huge problem."

"Who's using?"

"Opioid addiction isn't, well, prejudiced, so to speak. Addiction doesn't fall only on the lower-income, the higher-income, or the middle-income folks. It's across the board. As we gather intel on who's using, who's selling, and so on, I've learned you can't judge a book by its cover."

"Maybe what I'm really asking is how hard-core drugs became such a problem in our community. How did we get here?"

"I date this back to the introduction of prescription painkillers like OxyContin, starting in the late 1990s or so. Doctors started writing prescriptions for these drugs but without any treatment plan for getting people weaned off. So a high school kid might get injured playing soccer and end up with a prescription for narcotics."

"Soccer injuries happen all the time. That must have been very common."

He nodded. "Very. The kid gets put on a onetime prescription for pain pills and, before you know it, he's hooked on opioids. That's not what the doctor intended. But that's what happened. So he goes back to the doctor, who says, 'No, I can't prescribe any more,' because the injury is healed. But the kid's brain is telling him that he's still in pain. The problem is, now he's an addict. So where does he go? He goes to the street."

"If I'm following what you're saying, that teenager became an illegal drug user, all because of that onetime prescription."

"Exactly. It's not the only way people get hooked, by any means, but I've seen that scenario, over and over."

"How big a problem is this?"

As Cochran shifted his legs, the chunky key ring on his belt jangled. "Huge. This is complicated, but in brief, maybe ten years ago, opioids were really becoming a problem. Oxy 80s, known as Big Boys on the street, were everywhere. People were crushing the pills to remove the time-release coating — the thing that was supposed to make them less addictive — and snorting them. One way the feds cracked down was by compiling a database that hooked together pharmacies, so law enforcement, from the DEA to the Hardwick PD, could see where those prescriptions came from. When those prescriptions dried up, that enormous black market of pills dried up, too. Now Big Boys are virtually nonexistent. You can't find them anywhere."

"Could you spell this out a little more for me?"

"You have to realize, drugs are a business, and that revolves, like any business, around supply and demand. The demand is from the addicts; they want to get high. When the supply of black-market pills was cut off, the demand was still there. That hadn't changed. People who are dealing drugs, and profiting, had to find a new supply of drugs to fill that demand. So the suppliers started flooding their market with heroin."

"I see." The office was getting warmer, and I shrugged my cardigan off my shoulders. "I know this sounds naive, but there's a lot of money in drugs?"

"An enormous amount. I've been told some dealers lace marijuana with opioids, to bring in new customers, so to speak. You have to remember the goal of the addict is to get high, which is not a rational activity. You or I would think that when there are a lot of overdose deaths in a short period of time in a localized area, users would get scared, because that means whatever substance is out there right then is likely mixed with something especially potent. But an addict actually told me that is not the case. They actually seek out where that intense drug came from."

"That's grim."

"It's no way to live your life." Cochran cleared his throat. "Here's the way I think about it. For a while, the zombie apocalypse was a big thing, and everything was zombie this and zombie that, television shows and so on. I see the opioid crisis as a modern-day zombie apocalypse. Drugs turn addicts into people nobody knows. They don't even know who they are anymore themselves. They're willing to do almost anything to get that high, regardless of who they hurt. The consequences don't matter. Family members are not family members to them anymore."

"Is there any way to encourage people to get treatment?"

"In my experience, I don't think you're going to get anybody to come forward who's using until they're ready to stop. These are extremely powerful drugs. Remember, maybe ten years ago, there was a police chief in Vermont, I forget the town now, who had a habit of pain pills?"

"Vaguely. I must have read about it or heard something on VPR."

"That chief had his officers get the pills from evidence. Eventually, he had an accident in a cruiser and ended up losing his job. There again, it's not a matter of economic status. It could be anybody."

"He encountered legal trouble, then. I imagine that happens frequently, before the user is really ready to quit using."

"All the time."

"So about recovery . . . I had a fascinating conversation with a nurse at the health center. She's a strong advocate for harm reduction. She believes that compassion, and ameliorating the stigma surrounding substance users, can play a significant role in getting people on the path to sobriety. I'm curious what you think about that approach."

"Sure, there's a place for compassion, and, sure, we shouldn't pick on anyone. But I would also argue that we've developed into a society of people who don't want to feel any pain. People need to realize that they have to take responsibility for themselves."

"I don't disagree."

"What I see, over and over, is that someone's drug problem becomes everyone else's problem. I agree, compassion is a good idea, but does that mean we should give every addict a free pass? No one plans to become a drug addict; we all know that. Addiction can come out of a onetime deal at a party where someone may not have even known what they were taking. But in my job I deal with the addict who breaks into the retired schoolteacher's house and steals fifty bucks from her cookie jar. He's now spread his problem to her house."

I glanced at the round clock hanging over the door. The time was nearly ten, and I needed to leave in a few minutes. "When I started asking harder questions about substance abuse, I hadn't realized how deep addiction goes. Like, how the person who broke into the teacher's house has connected that teacher, in a way, to someone using heroin. For that matter, thinking through this more, heroin has to be imported, too; it's not like Vermont cheese. Once you start unraveling this problem, maybe it goes on and on."

Cochran pointed out that Hardwick has three state highways running through it: Routes 14 and 15 and, in East Hardwick, Route 16. "Those highways bring in a lot of people from out of town. Sure, some of them are here to visit Great-Aunt Myrna or whomever, but a lot of them aren't." He stretched out his legs.

I couldn't help but notice how different were the tools of our occupations: he had a belt with a handgun and a Taser; I carried a backpack with a laptop and books. But we were both responsible to the public. "There are a lot of pieces to this job, aren't there? A lot going on under the surface?"

"This is just the tip of it. I get the usual phone calls about speeding and barking dogs, but we're also dealing with things that are so much bigger than someone who's doing five miles per hour over the speed limit on a local street. You asked about the Woodbury case? I've lived here my whole life. I have never seen anything of that magnitude. You certainly didn't see anything like that over marijuana."

I thanked him for his time and walked out through the metal doors. The cold stabbed the infection in my jaw, and I cupped my lower face with my hand as I walked home. A dank fog shrouded the river and wrapped the buildings in a gauzy scrim. To warm up, I stopped into the co-op and poured myself a cup of coffee in the upstairs café, then stood in front of the window, rubbing that sore spot on my jaw and thinking about what Cochran had said: that addiction transforms people into empty shells of themselves.

"What's up with you?" June Jenkins called across the empty café from the stove behind the counter. In the open kitchen, she pulled out a huge sheet of steaming scones from the oven. She had dyed her hair turquoise. "You look like you're in pain."

"Failed root canal."

"Oooo," she commiserated. "Sounds awful. What happened? Cavity?"

"Injury. Years ago, I dropped a piece of firewood on it. Eric had stacked the wood in a pile higher than my head. A piece I pulled out slipped from my mitten and hit my tooth." The coffee was too hot for my aching mouth. "The tooth took years to die, and I didn't know until I got a raging infection."

With a spatula, June slid the scones on a plate. "You can stick a cigarette in that gap and carry around a can of Bud Light."

"Go ahead and laugh."

"You'll just look like you're smoking crack." The phone rang. "Hello. Buffalo Mountain Co-op Café."

I set the nearly full cup of coffee in the dirty dish bin and left. In a depressing downpour, I cinched my hood and walked up the hill, past the empty school ball field, and through the cemetery. The polished granite tombstones glistened in the rain. A pestilent rot had grown in me, and I hadn't even realized it. Soon there would be an ugly, gaping hole in my mouth. I would look like the saddest of the down-and-out.

I followed the path to our house along the hydrangeas, the green stalks faded to brown, their blossoms skeletons. At our porch, I stood on the top step beneath the roof, leaning against our house. The rain had morphed into sleet, accumulating icily on curled-over brussels sprouts in my garden, the leaves already crinkled by hard frosts. Beyond the cemetery, the village appeared as a shellacked, two-dimensional collage, ranging from sooty to silver. The first night I lived in Vermont as a wide-eyed college freshman, I dragged my bed beside the bare window and fell asleep staring at the stars. I believed then, as I still do, that I had found my place. I love the Vermont of needle-like steeples and sweeping hayfields, the Green Mountain Club and Ben & Jerry's coupling of ice cream and left-leaning politics, town meetings and packed pie breakfasts, the state whose motto celebrates Freedom and Unity. But my conversation with Cochran had ripped up one corner of that glossy covering and exposed a Vermont that I hadn't seen.

A Hundred Billion Doses

My brother, Nik, and his girlfriend, Jess, celebrated Christmas with a ham dinner at our dining room table, followed by hours of Hearts games alternating with trivia. In our cozy living room, Nik sprawled on the couch with Acer on his chest. I lay on the floor. "Remember when our old Jeep broke down in the Grand Canyon," he said, "and Dad took it apart in the campground?"

I laughed. "I'd forgotten that."

"How could you forget? You know how many times he fixed that thing on those trips?"

"Do you remember how you always complained about setting up the tent?"

"Wrong again. You were the whiner, sis."

In the evening, the five of us and their dogs walked in a steady snowfall. With almost no one about, the road crew had the holiday off, too, and the unplowed streets were covered with four inches of pristine white. Under a streetlight, my brother tipped his head back. "Remember as kids we used to wonder where flakes come from? Somehow 'from the clouds' didn't seem like a good enough answer for such a marvel."

Gabriela spread her arms wide and spun around on one boot. "It's Christmas gift snow."

After the holidays, January's cold sank in. I wore winter boots on my walks around town. People left their cars running in grocery store parking lots while they shopped. The fire in the woodstove never went out, and the cats sprawled with their paws outstretched, sleeping all day before its warmth. What had also changed was that after my conversation with Cochran, I looked differently at Vermont's bucolic facade. One Saturday on my way to the post office, I glanced through the windows of a black SUV with New York license plates parked beside the Laundromat, wondering what had brought its occupants to town. Family ski vacation? Or something else entirely? With the glass in the rear windows tinted black, all I spied through the windshield was a silver metal mug in the console, which might have meant anything.

One afternoon, reading my library email, I chanced upon a press release announcing that Christina Nolan, the United States attorney for Vermont, had recently made a short film with a man named Justin Goulet — no relation to Meg Goulet — who had gone to jail and was now in long-term recovery. In the documentary, Nolan said that speaking openly about addiction and sharing stories of recovery was necessary to combat drug abuse. I puzzled over this approach; I expected a prosecutor to voice a hard line, not focus on lessening stigma. Her office requested paper letters of inquiry, not emails, so I wrote one, introducing myself as a small-town librarian, and asked if she would help me understand how Vermont is dealing with illegal drugs. On my way home, I dropped the envelope at the post office.

Three days later, I was washing up the breakfast dishes when a Burlington number flashed across the screen of my phone. A woman from Nolan's office thanked me for my letter and said that Nolan wanted to meet me.

"I'd appreciate that."

"Does next Tuesday, 10:00 a.m., work for you?"

"I'll make it work."

That Tuesday morning, I parked on the top floor of a Burlington garage, zipped up my coat, and tugged my scarf nearly to my eyes before stepping out of my car into the raw wind that plagues the Queen City in the winter months. While some years much of the lake remains as open water all winter, the whole expanse was already frozen that January, a great plain of stark, snowy white. Rushing down the garage stairs to the street, my heavy winter boot slipped on the last step. I lurched forward and nearly fell, saving myself by grabbing the metal railing.

I hurried through the brick-paved Church Street Marketplace shopping district on my way to the six-story Burlington Federal Building, a large structure for such a small city. I had my ID checked, entered through a metal detector, and was directed to an elevator.

When the door slid open, a petite woman, not much taller than I am, in a dark blue suit and a short, unfussy haircut was walking toward me with her hand outstretched. "Christina Nolan," she said warmly, shaking my hand and looking directly into my eyes. "Thank you for reaching out."

Nolan led me down the hall to her office and gestured for me to sit on one of the long couches on either side of a coffee table. Her expansive office, with its two walls of windows, peered over the city. "You're a librarian you said? What is it you're looking for?"

I took a deep breath. "I'll try to condense this long story. A year ago, a man in town, who was connected to my library and was a known drug user, committed suicide. His death rippled into the community, from his family and friends to the first responders, my trustees and, well, me." Even as I spoke, I realized I was using Shauna's words about her brother's death when he was hit by a pickup; the suffering that ensued from his death, she had said, spread out so far. "In hindsight, I know fear overshadowed my actions. Since then, I've often wondered if I might have been able to offer this man some help, if I had been more informed about drug abuse."

"Are you asking about opioids, specifically, or addiction more generally?"

"Well, at first, I was completely focused on opioid abuse. But I kept asking questions; I participated in a Department of Libraries statewide Narcan training and met with medical practitioners and people in recovery. Gradually, I began to realize that I needed to look at addiction itself."

"It sounds like you're on the right track. Often, the media only sees the opioid crisis, but addiction as a whole is the larger problem. Right now, for instance, we're seeing a rise in the use of meth, a devastating drug that isn't particularly on the public radar."

Between us, a low table displayed a glass jar shaped like a goldfish bowl, filled with hard yellow candies in cellophane wrappers.

Nolan continued. "First, I'll emphasize that being addicted isn't a crime; it's what people do to maintain their habit that gets them in trouble with the law."

"Of course."

"I always mention that, because sometimes that's a blurry place. Second, the goal of this office is to reduce supply and reduce demand. That's a succinct version of a complicated approach to combating drug abuse. To reduce supply, we hold people accountable for their actions. For some offenders, I recommend jail time. For others, treatment is more appropriate, so we've focused on making that path more accessible than it was in the past."

"Is treatment part of the 'reduce demand' approach?"

"Absolutely. We can't afford to look at addiction with tunnel vision. We should be just as focused, if not more so, on prevention as we are on punishment. As a state, we had to really step up our approach when drugs like fentanyl appeared, because we saw people rapidly descend into terrible addictions, and the overdose rate skyrocketed. That crisis forced us to quickly create a new approach, based on collaboration, such as between law enforcement and treatment. In the past, that hasn't happened."

"Why not? That seems like such an obvious partnership."

"I'll just say, well, the right and left hands weren't always talking with each other before. As a librarian, you've now participated in this plan, when you were trained to administer Narcan. Pulling in public librarians is one piece of the larger strategy. We also focused on opening up the dialogue about addiction. Part of our challenge, as a society, is to overcome the fear and stigma surrounding addiction."

"That approach, which I first saw in your documentary with Justin Goulet, is what led me to you. It isn't what I expected from a prosecutor, honestly."

Nolan tipped her head slightly to one side, considering her words. "We're never going to understand addiction if we don't start speaking openly about it. I wanted people to see a real person who had struggled with substance abuse, who had done time in a federal prison and had gone on to a live a full life. Now Justin's a business owner. Every year, we lose people in this state, and in this country, to drug abuse — lives that don't need to be lost. But as long as someone's alive, there's always hope. I can't emphasize hope enough; this isn't a political speech, or a pep talk, but a philosophy that underlies all my work."

I glanced out the window. Across the street, pigeons huddled on a brick ledge beneath a roof overhang. "Like so many people, I have personal experience with addiction." I looked back at Nolan, who was watching me attentively. "And I agree with what you're saying, but I also see a lot of fear surrounding addiction — and opioid abuse in particular. I'm from a small, rural town that recently had two homicides. I'm sure you know about this."

"Yes."

"Although I might wish otherwise, I can't just brush off that fear as if it doesn't matter. Woodbury has had so many break-ins now that folks created a Facebook group to keep an eye on their community."

"That fear is legitimate. No one wants to live in towns where people are murdered. No one wants to live in towns, either, that are terrorized by petty crime. But I'm going to pose a challenge to you."

"What's that?"

"Think about this. Fear also feeds stigma, and stigma blinds us. Yes, addiction is destructive. Yes, we should be wary. In this office, I see the worst crimes in Vermont, like human trafficking and child pornography. But I know if we don't face what's in front of us, we can't address those problems."

"I'm not trying to blind myself, nor am I trying to be stupid, but how does lessening the stigma of drug abuse actually help combat addiction? Many people would argue the opposite: that if you try to understand substance abusers, you're going soft on crime. You're making addiction more acceptable."

"Categorically, no. I would never normalize an activity like heroin use. But the more we understand addiction, the more effective we'll be at eradicating it. I'll point you back to Justin, who served his time and is now helping other people. I also insist that addiction is not a given in our society. We don't need to accept it as an inevitability."

"That's an incredibly hopeful vision."

"I'm an optimistic person — a glass-half-full, not half-empty person."

I slipped my scarf from my neck and wound the threadbare cloth through my fingers. "I've always considered myself an optimistic person, too, but once I really started digging into the connections between addiction and society, my views changed. It seems to me that you could lock up every local dealer, but heroin would keep flowing in. The power of these substances, from what I gather, is overwhelming. This isn't just weed someone is growing in their backyard."

"That's true. Dealing illicit substances is a multimillion-dollar business. In Vermont, we're not just going after the local dealers. We're also doing everything we can to hold responsible those suppliers who profit from others' suffering and deaths. Sometimes that means prosecuting local people; sometimes that means going at much deeper sources."

"What do you mean by that? Going after gangs from other states?"

"Absolutely. However, overprescribing physicians and narcotics manufacturers are as much responsible for the proliferation of opioids as dealers from Springfield, Massachusetts. That process is going to unwind through the court system for a very long time to come."

Snow began to fall lightly over the red-brick city, flake by flake. "Listening to you, I keep thinking of when I visited Brattleboro last summer with my daughter and her friend, who are both fourteen. I used to live in that town, and I ran into an old friend in the co-op. While we were talking, I looked through one of the large front windows and saw a man approaching the girls. They wore backpacks, so maybe he thought these otherwise clean-cut girls were runaways. I ran outside, but the man had disappeared into the crowd." I raised my eyes from my gray-and-blue scarf and met Nolan's gaze. "When I was a college student in Brattleboro, I lived alone and walked all over. But now? I was in the co-op for all of ten minutes, and a stranger approached my two teenage girls. I looked at that town harder and began to see how its character had changed. The bathrooms at the co-op are now locked, because of repeated overdoses. I see an itinerant, somewhat sketchy crowd that didn't seem visible before, if it was even there. I started wondering, *What the heck is happening here?*"

Barely perceptibly, Nolan winced.

I waited. When she didn't answer, I continued, "When I look now, I see changes like that in different degrees all over Vermont."

"I'll say this. All of Vermont has suffered from opioid abuse, but Windham County has been hit especially hard. Dealers can drive an hour north up I-91 from Massachusetts cities and double their money, since supplies are lower in Vermont. That profit is an enormous draw."

"I find this unsettling. I mean, I'm a mother to two young women." Glancing at that glass bowl of butterscotch candies, I quelled an impulse to reach in.

"It's frightening, for mothers and everyone else. But again, I'm going to challenge you not to be consumed by that fear. This isn't a problem one person, or even a handful of people, are going to solve. We need many, many people all working together, from judges to preventionists to librarians." She gestured to me with one hand. "There's a part for everyone here, for those who choose it."

"I guess that's the perennial existential question," I said, standing up, "isn't it? How do you act in the world?"

Nolan stood up, too. "It's a question worth asking."

"I doubt I'll solve that conundrum today. But thank you for your time."

We walked down the hall and stopped at the elevator door. "These are important conversations, for you, hopefully, but also for me."

She pressed the button for the lobby. "One more thing — when you said you had personal knowledge of addiction, maybe you should think of that as an asset. As a strength."

"Isn't there an old adage about how your strengths are your weaknesses?"

"Right, but only if you use that strength. That's the ticket."

We shook hands. Then I stepped into the elevator, and the door slid shut behind me.

∞

I drove the long way home, winding along the Winooski River on Route 2 toward Waterbury, where I stopped at the Stowe Street Café and ordered a double espresso. In the early afternoon, the café was empty but for two elderly women, yakking over lunch plates strewn with sandwich crusts and parsley sprigs. In a sunny corner, I sat down and scrawled a few words in my notebook about my conversation with Nolan: reduce supply, reduce demand, accountability, crime, fear.

Still chatting, the women stood and zipped up mid-calf down overcoats. As they walked slowly toward the door, the young man behind the counter set down his phone and called out, "Have a lovely afternoon, ladies! Hope your lunch was up to par."

The taller woman spread a gardenia-patterned scarf over her white curls and bow-tied it beneath her chin. "That curried chicken was exactly what the doctor ordered to keep the winter blues away!" She opened the door and stepped out with her friend, a frosty gust blowing into the café.

Suddenly ravenous, I walked over to the glass-fronted pastry display and ordered a slice of triple-layer chocolate cake.

"Black forest," the young man said. "My fav." A thumbnail-sized emerald heart was tattooed on his collarbone. With a silver knife, he cut me a hefty piece, then used the side of the blade to scoop syrupy cherries on the plate. As he handed over change from my twenty, his phone rang. "Excuse me." He stepped back and perched on a stool, heels hooked over a rung, whispering into the phone.

At my corner table, I took a bite of the cake. As the buttery frosting melted in my mouth, I suddenly saw addiction not as stasis — a word or a condition — but as an insatiable, never-ending desire. I set down my fork and wrote in my notebook, "hunger."

The first time I had slipped into that blur of drunkenness was the Thanksgiving I was thirteen, when I managed to drink glass after glass of champagne and white wine without any adult noticing. While my parents napped after dinner, I wandered outside in the silvery autumn twilight, exuberant, heady with my discovery. Right then, I was smitten.

At that sunny table, I ate the cake, bit by bit, relishing the slightly bitter chocolate. When I finished, I set my empty demitasse and frosting-smeared plate and fork on the counter. Phone still pressed to his ear, the barista gave me a thumbs-up. As I headed for the door, I heard him say, "You rock, gorgeous woman." I turned around, but he was speaking into his phone, his gaze upward, smiling.

∽

Back home, my daughters were packing their bags with extra gloves and socks. My brother had ski passes and invited them to his house for the weekend. I dug into the stash of garlic I had grown in my garden last summer and filled a small paper bag with a dozen heads. "Take these for Nik." I handed the bag to Molly.

Kneeling on the floor, she tucked the bag into her duffel. "We'll be back Sunday night, Mom. Think you can stay out of trouble for a few days?"

"Possibly. You better leave soon. It's going to be dark in an hour or so."

"My car has headlights. I can actually drive in the dark."

Gabriela added, "Yeah, dude. Headlights."

"Watch for deer along the way. Text me when you get there. And have fun!"

Gabriela scrolled through her phone. "Let's play my music on the way."

Hefting their bags over their shoulders, the girls headed out to Molly's black Honda. I tugged on my coat again and grabbed a pair of skis from the deck. Molly loaded the hatch while Gabriela arranged the bags on the backseat, then buckled into the passenger seat. I opened the door and hugged my youngest. "Drive safely," I cautioned Molly.

"Always!" She started the engine.

They drove away, waving at me through the unrolled windows.

I hurried inside, then stood beside the woodstove, relishing its warmth. For a moment, I closed my eyes, imagining a bird's-eye view of the highways I had traveled that day. From that height, any vehicle or person was inseparable from the landscape of stony mountain, serpentine river, and snow-buried field.

I lifted Acer and rubbed his white chin, rubbing with his throat purr. His brother, Tar Leo, wandered in and meowed, eager for dinner. I fed the cats, then opened my laptop at the kitchen table. For the first time, I began to see how Hardwick and Woodbury were another waystation on a modern Silk Road. Where and when did this all start? Curious about the historical roots of substance abuse, I opened a browser window and began reading about the saga of addiction that stretches back, at least, to the Sumerians, who named the opium poppy *hul gil* — the "joy plant" — around 3,400 BCE.

Although poppy varieties grow in Vermont gardens, the opium poppy, which contains the most potent narcotic, thrives best in a temperate, dry climate; its delicate roots prefer sandy loam and long hours of sunlight. Easily identified by its long, pale-green, jagged-edged leaves and gracefully drooping head, the poppy is relatively easy to grow, attracts few pests or diseases, demands no costly irrigation or pesticides, and seeds prolifically. In the field, poppies grow well with other plants, such as beans, peas, or tobacco — an added benefit to their farmers.

Opium has been transported — by pocket, camel, clipper ship, and airplane — for thousands of years. When Columbus connected continents, more than potatoes and tomatoes exchanged hands. Opium from the Middle East united with the Native American pipe, a cultural swap with disastrous consequences. Inhaled, opium is absorbed into the blood far more rapidly and efficiently than by ingesting. By the nineteenth century, opium dens materialized around the globe.

In that century, China and Great Britain went to war over this black substance made from the sappy resin of poppy flowers. Chinese commissioner Lin Zexu wrote to Queen Victoria in 1839, decrying how British opium smuggling in China instigated widespread addiction and a resultant malaise. Great Britain, Lin Zexu wrote, had prohibited opium on its home soil "with the utmost strictness and severity: this is a strong proof that you know full well how hurtful it is to mankind."

My phone buzzed. "Made it to NH," from Gabriela, flashed across the screen, followed by emojis of snowflakes and smiling faces. "NH mountains are way cooler than Vermont."

"Have fun!!" I typed back and added heart emojis.

I closed my laptop, stood, and stretched. On the stove, I heated olive oil in a pan and tossed in three popcorn kernels. When they burst, I added half a cup of the little golden beads. While the corn popped and dinged against the lid, I dipped my fingers into that jar of kernels. How differently these two crops, opium and maize, had imprinted on human history. Over centuries, maize had been nurtured by family farmers from a wild plant to a domesticated crop, feeding entire civilizations in the Americas. Likewise, opium was often cultivated in small plots, but this flower was propagated not for the dinner table but for destruction.

When the popping stopped, I dumped the fluffy kernels in a bowl, sprinkled salty black garlic over the pile, then sat at the kitchen table and opened my laptop again. In the late 1800s, pharmacists dispensed over-the-counter medications containing opium for nearly every malady, including elixirs for colicky babies. In the early twentieth century, in response to escalating rates of addiction, the federal government attempted to crack down on the free-flowing substances, passing the Harrison Narcotics Tax Act of 1914 — controversial legislation that confirmed the national perception that narcotics users are criminals rather than casualties of a disease. Harry Anslinger, the nation's first commissioner of the Federal Bureau of Narcotics and an unabashed racist, laid the groundwork for contemporary drug laws targeted specifically at Black Americans. Possessing or distributing crack cocaine, for instance, a substance used disproportionately by Blacks, incurs far greater mandatory prison sentences than powdered cocaine, more frequently used by whites, although the chemical composition is nearly identical.

I loaded the woodstove, brushed my teeth, then turned off the lights and went upstairs to bed. The house was silent. Lying in my dark room, my mind drifted among images of warships from the 1800s, wreathed in smoke from firing cannons, to smoky nightclubs where Lady Day serenaded rapt listeners with "Strange Fruit." Unable to sleep, I reached over to the window and pushed the curtain aside. In the amber streetlight, snow sifted down, sparkling as it landed in the road. I left the curtain parted for the night and fell asleep staring at the falling snow.

In the morning, I woke before dawn and pulled the quilts over my face. During the night, the woodstove always burned down to embers. On the bookshelf, Acer sat gnawing on the pineapple plant. "Hey," I said, gently. "Knock it off, little cat." I rose and fed the cats breakfast. Then I scraped the coals into a pile in the woodstove and added kindling. Flames whooshed up the chimney. The day promised more snow, a good opportunity to keep reading.

From my desk, I picked up the book Katie Whitaker had recommended, Travis Rieder's *In Pain: A Bioethicist's Personal Struggle with Opioids*. When his foot was nearly severed after a motorcycle accident, Rieder was prescribed massive amounts of narcotics — drugs he came to know very well. I sat on the couch with my coffee and the book.

In 1995, the American Pain Society categorized pain as the "fifth vital sign," declaring that "quality care means that pain is measured and treated." The decision encouraged many physicians to prescribe narcotic pain relief abundantly. If a physician believes that opioids are a pathway to healing, why not prescribe these medications? But unlike other vital signs — blood pressure, heart and respiratory rate, and temperature — no objective measurement for pain exists, beyond the evaluation of the sufferer and a blurry scale of one to ten.

In 1996, Purdue Pharma, a corporation owned and controlled by the Sackler family and a major contributor to the APS, introduced OxyContin, a time-release version of oxycodone. Purdue directed their hundreds of sales reps to aggressively market this drug as a less addictive opioid.

The plan worked: opioid prescriptions skyrocketed. But Oxy-Contin, as is now well known, is phenomenally addictive. Many users bypassed the time-release feature by crushing the pill and snorting or injecting the powder for an intense high. As increasing numbers of people became addicted, more and more companies jumped on the money wagon, manufacturing and distributing massive quantities of narcotics to alleviate pains ranging from work-place injuries to aging, flooding the country with opioid prescriptions. Hundreds of thousands of people ended up addicted to pain medication, and a superabundance of these pills appeared in the hands of people who didn't have a prescription.

In 2016, in response to skyrocketing rates of opioid addiction nationwide, "the CDC took the unprecedented action of releasing its own guidelines for prescribing opioids, urging doctors not to see opioids as first-line therapy for non-cancer chronic pain patients and to use opioids only sparingly, in low doses, for short amounts of time for treatment of acute pain." As legal prescriptions tightened, demand for black-market opioids increased. With pills increasingly pricier, substantially cheaper heroin flowed in to fill that demand. What I was reading matched what Aaron Cochran described in our region. Now heroin is cut with other drugs, including fentanyl, which is "fifty to one hundred times more powerful than morphine," and carfentanil, an elephant tranquilizer so formidable that a dose the size of a salt grain can be fatal.

I closed the Rieder book and opened my laptop. Nolan had mentioned legal battles. Across the country, I read, as states and cities struggled with the human and economic challenges caused by opioid abuse, lawsuits piled up against pharmaceutical companies and distributors. Eventually, a federal judge combined approximately two thousand lawsuits against Purdue Pharma and the Sackler family that were presided over by Judge Dan Polster in Cleveland, Ohio.

In October 2018, Vermont's attorney general, T. J. Donovan, filed a lawsuit against Purdue Pharma, which alleged that "by the mid-2000s, Purdue had succeeded in drastically changing medical and public opinion about opioids." Formerly prescribed only as postsurgical, traumatic, or palliative cancer-relief pain medication, opioids had become a common treatment for everyday pain, without scientific evidence to support any safety claims. The state alleged that Purdue knew — and exploited — the addictive dangers of opioids.

I stood at the window facing the cemetery, staring out as a north wind gusted snow whirls through the tombstones. The previous summer, my mother, an eighty-two-year-old retired nurse, endured an umbilical hernia repair after she had a cancerous kidney removed. In the hours after her surgery, OxyContin flowed through her veins to alleviate the pain she could hardly endure, even with the drug. When my father left the recovery room for coffee, my mother clasped my hand between the bedrails, whispering, "I think I'm on the way out." She wasn't. On that rainy afternoon in northern New Mexico, opioids provided her body with space to heal.

Wind howled around my house. I remembered what Christina Nolan said — that a weakness can also be a strength — but isn't the reverse also true? The drugs that alleviated my mother's pain have also caused untold pain to so many people.

In the 2000s, OxyContin grossed Purdue Pharma more than a billion dollars annually.

∽

I still hadn't answered the question of whether addiction was a disease or bad behavior. But what made me care so much? I knew I would never discover a definitive answer — addiction is not caused by any bacteria with a Latin name — but the ramifications appeared significant. Disease relieves the user of culpability. Choice holds the user accountable. But what if I was asking the wrong question? What if addiction tangles together disease and volition? Framing addiction as a disease, or not, began to seem to me a reductively simple, either / or way of looking at a problem with many sides.

While another little silver pot of coffee brewed on the kitchen stove, I stooped down and petted Tar Leo, who was curled in a blanket-lined box beneath the table. Then I added milk to my coffee and sat down with another library book.

Katie had also recommended that I read Hungarian-born Dr. Gabor Maté, whose classic book, *In the Realm of Hungry Ghosts: Close Encounters with Addiction*, chronicles his experiences working with people suffering from severe substance abuse in Vancouver. Maté stresses that a drug-addicted brain is an ailing brain. Repeated and persistent use of certain substances, such as cocaine, rewires the human brain. *"These are drugs for which animals and humans will develop craving and that they will seek compulsively."* (Maté's italics.) The more severe the addiction, the greater the impact on the brain. But Maté also emphasizes the multitude of factors contributing to addiction. The world of the addict matters. "In the real world choice, will, and responsibility are not absolute and unambiguous concepts. People choose, decide, and act in a context . . ."

With my laptop, I sat beside our woodstove on the round red rug in our living room. Acer laid beside me, stretching out his front paws while I rubbed his ebony head. The word *context* — the gray zone of human life — had perplexed me for years. Surely, I thought, substances like nicotine and morphine, or Hershey's bars, by themselves do not cause addiction any more than a bottle of Jack Daniel's creates an alcoholic. Rieder developed a physical tolerance for opioids and experienced miserable withdrawal symptoms, including a crippling depression, but he never had a crazed compulsion to consume opioids; in other words, he never developed an addiction. Does this mean that people who abuse drugs are fragile? Inherently immoral? Who develops an addiction? And why?

I would never definitively know why I developed a drinking problem, and my friend Diane, who in many ways had a much harder life than mine, did not. Katie had pointed out to me that much about addiction is not yet known. On an even more profound level, too, I know much of our lives is an enigma — charming and intriguing at times and utterly baffling and infuriating at others.

I pushed my laptop away and lay on my back. Through the soot-stained glass door of the woodstove, I watched the flickering orange flames. Uncertainty aside, there was plenty we did know. Mesmerized by the fire, I couldn't stop pondering lines in a lawsuit filed by the Massachusetts attorney general Maura Healey against Purdue Pharmaceuticals. CEO Craig Landau's notes cited in the lawsuit read:

There are:
   Too many Rxs being written
   Too high a dose
   For too long
   For conditions that often don't require them
   By doctors who lack the requisite training in how to use
      them appropriately.

Healey wrote, "The opioid epidemic is not a mystery to the people who started it."

∾

In the late afternoon, Molly called. "Epic skiing!"

"I'm so glad to hear that. You're back at Nik's house?"

"Yeah. We're making dinner. You want to talk to him?"

"Yeah, but first — have a good night. Give your little sister a hug."

I closed my laptop, set it aside, and sprawled on my back on the rug.

"Yo," my brother said. "The powder on the slopes was one for the record books. What'd you do today?"

"I've been home reading. Petting the cats. You know how I told you about that suicide at my library?"

"Last winter? Yeah, the girls said you'd been bugged by that."

In the background, I heard Molly call out, "I said she was obsessed!"

I sighed. "Take that with a great big grain of whatever."

"I get it. What were you reading about? Death is generally the endgame of suicide. Research it all you want, Ms. Librarian, but there's nowhere to go."

"It's not death I was researching. I live next to a cemetery. I have a pretty good picture of where that story ends."

He laughed. "You and those cemeteries."

"Look, if you're not going to be serious, hang up, and I'll talk to the cats instead."

"Oh, I'll humor you. If it's not death you're researching, tell me it's my summer vacation."

"Not likely. No, I've been reading about addiction, and I'm beginning to realize how little I understood about the topic."

"I find that somewhat unbelievable."

"The thing is, I used to think about addiction just in terms of me — like, why was I so messed up? I never stepped outside myself and saw that addiction isn't just my own personal plight. When Baker died, I started wondering what made this opioid crisis so enormous. I mean, drugs and booze have always been around, but how did this get so big and so god-awful?"

"Jess!" Nik hollered. "Turn on the oven to 350! — I'm here, sis. I got sidetracked by a gorgeous-looking steak. Now I'm all ears for you. Crisis? Anything different? And you concluded what?"

"I don't have any more answers than anyone else, of course, but I'm just going to keep talking, because you know about addiction, too, and, besides, there's no one else but the cats here, and they are lousy sounding boards."

"Fair enough. Continue. I'm just going to kick back this recliner," he grunted, "and put my feet up."

"At the risk of boring you — here's what I think is different. One, the drugs got more potent. I mean, mainlining heroin was always a bad idea, but Oxy and fentanyl and carfentanil are bigger and badder drugs."

"I get that."

"The other thing is, drug dealing has always been a major business — the mob is hardly small potatoes — but this crisis was created by corporations with an intentional strategy to get people hooked on Oxy, all for billions in profit. *The Washington Post* published a piece recently about court-ordered released data. Over an eight-year period, the country was flooded with a hundred billion doses of Oxy and hydrocodone. That's staggering."

"A hundred billion doses? How do you even make that number meaningful, beyond, WTF?"

"Think of it this way. The CDC estimates that two hundred thousand Americans have died from overdoses related to the Sacklers' OxyContin since 1999. Vermont's population is around 625,000. So proportionally, an overdose death nationally — not just an overdose, but a fatality — numbers one out of every three Vermonters."

"Damn. Kind of like Great Big Tobacco."

"The girls told you I visited the US attorney for Vermont? Christina Nolan?"

"They mentioned something."

"I was impressed by her determination to reduce stigma around drug abuse. She really seemed to have a huge heart. But does she stand a chance?"

"This is capitalism with a giant capital *C* that you, Ms. Librarian, are not ever, ever going to change or affect. Your daughters would like you to move on. Jess, I'd rub that with cumin, chili, and garlic salt. Maybe some butter?"

"Am I interrupting your culinary lessons?"

"I can do more than one thing at a time. I'd also like to mention that if you fed your kids meat occasionally and not just that vegetarian hippie shit, they might actually want to come home . . ."

"That's super helpful."

"Look, I'll give you some advice. Why don't you go out and get laid? Grow up and get a Tinder account. Why are you always stuck with your head in a book? It's like you're still ten and reading those goddamn Trixie Belden books."

"I so wanted to be Trixie Belden. She had a fantastic brother."

I heard him spit out beer as he laughed. "Is this an existential crisis you're having?"

"Aren't existential crises supposed to be growth points?"

"Screw that. Why can't this family just aim for some happiness? Hey, kid, beer me again!"

I lay down on the couch with the phone to my ear, watching snow drift down lazily through the windows. Snow-globe snow we called it, as if the frozen water was nothing more than little flecks imprisoned in a tchotchke.

Nik cleared his throat. "The existential crisis? This is about that guy in the library? What's his name? The cobbler? The cooper?"

"Baker. Are you even faintly interested in this?" I asked.

"I am, actually. I'm even putting my coat back on and taking the phone outside with me. For some air and privacy, because I don't think you've cleared the woods yet." Nik gasped into the phone as he started up the hill. "Jesus, I'm getting old."

"You're two and a half years younger than me. You better not be getting old yet."

"Here's the thing about existential crises. There's a point to them. You have to learn from them."

"I have."

"Yeah? What'd you learn?"

"So a year ago, I thought addiction was a blight on the soul — someone's personal failing. But now, I've learned that, for many people, addiction has a genetic component."

I heard him swallow. "I'm aware. Any other brilliant insights, sis?"

"Take that genetic component and pair it with an unhealthy environment. You grow up with drug users, or hang with heavy drinkers, and you're likely to normalize that behavior, take it in as your own. So that's genes and behavior. Then add the mixture of institutionalized racism, poverty, and trauma."

"What you're saying is, don't be so quick to judge?"

"I'm saying I fucked up. My attitude was, you junkie, get out of the library. How much more of a moral high horse could I have gotten on? I could have said, *I've been there, man, but I got out, and you can, too.* After all I went through when Eric lost his shit, and I was alone with the kids, how did I turn my back on someone in need? Remember how my neighbors kept driving by, rubbernecking?"

"Still pissed off?"

"Yeah, I'm still pissed off, but at myself now, too. What the hell is the point of all this misery if I didn't learn something from it? If I just turn around and do the same thing to someone else?"

"Guess what, sis? The world's not a perfect place. Also, you were a boozer. You never used heroin. You didn't know, right? The real challenge, of course, is putting knowledge into action. The mind might be clearer than the heart." He breathed in heavily. "Damn, it's snowing again. Can you fucking believe it? We're far from being out of the winter woods yet."

HEART

eleven

The Black Dog

A few weeks later, I was driving to work along Route 14 when, just as I passed M&M Beverage at the edge of town where the town neighborhoods end and the road curves through a swamp, *I want a drink* scurried through my mind. Years ago, I stopped into M&M every week to buy bottles and then boxes of wine. As I drove, I remembered the warmth of wine in my mouth, the sweetness of Cabernet, how wine promises happiness but often delivers misery. Breathless, I swerved to the side of the highway and pulled over at a roadside spring known as the water tub.

I put the car in park and gripped the steering wheel with both hands. *What the hell?* I thought. *What's happening?*

I hadn't argued with anyone. I wasn't worried about how to portion my paycheck into the mortgage and heating bills, wondering how much would remain for groceries. I wasn't obsessing over my ex or weeping over the demise of our once-conjoined lives. But if I couldn't blame this fleeting thought on anxiety or unhappiness, then I had to admit that the desire to drink might simply reside in me, true as the compulsion to lie down at the end of a long day, or as keen as hunger after a day hiking in the mountains.

I got out of my tiny Toyota. Trembling, I stared at water running from the spring's metal pipe, splashing in the cement basin lined with dirt-flecked ice. A log truck sped by. Once again, winter seemed unsurvivable. Despite its frosty, enchanting beauty, the season is too damn long and lonely. Overhead, in the narrow cut of the mountain pass, the sky was an ashen sliver, a jagged wound flanked by the uneven line of treetops.

In the dim January light, I breathed the cold air, remembering how Meg Goulet pointed to her head moments after we met and told me about the scars and metal screws she'll carry forever. Why had I spent so many years pretending that drinking hadn't scarred me?

Across Route 14, a metal clip clanged against an aluminum flag-pole in front of a home surrounded by acres of woods. Closing my eyes, I listened to the dirge-like banging as the wind stung my eyelids and ears. I remembered how on Molly's fourth birthday, after she had gone to sleep, I gathered up the wrapping paper from her pres-ents and stuffed the papers into the roaring woodstove. "What are you doing?" Eric shouted at me. "Trying to burn down the house? Maybe you just should go ahead and do that. Put us all out of our misery." The next morning, when Molly was looking through her presents, she couldn't find three tiny cloth dolls I had bought her. Inadvertently, I had incinerated those dolls with their wrappings. She said nothing except, "I still have one." I didn't respond. How much lower could I sink?

I was filled with such shame. How could I, a woman who appeared to have so many privileges — an education, a thriving business, a house, a hundred acres, and motherhood — struggle with a drink-ing problem? What the fuck was the matter with me?

∽

Shivering alone by the roadside, I wrapped my arms around my torso. I'd forgotten my hat and lost my scarf.

For years, I had used a small, heavy-bottomed glass for alcohol, which I kept separate from the tumblers my family used. When Molly was four, she called that glass "Mama's cup." After I had been sober for a few months, I slipped the glass in my knitting bag when I was headed out alone to get groceries. That afternoon, I pulled the car over on a wooded stretch of back road, stood on the shoulder, and threw the glass as far as I could into the forest.

When I was a grad student, stretched out on the rug beside the woodstove in the trailer Eric and I had rented in rural Washington

State, I read a John Updike novel about a young mother who was drinking sugar and whiskey and drowned her baby daughter in the bathtub. The act stayed with the woman her entire life.

I opened my eyes as a semi roared down the curving mountain pass. When the truck and the line of traffic trailing it disappeared around the curve, the roadside was again just me and the clanging metal clip, the water running from that pipe, and all around the forest, with its bare trees and snow-covered ground. Peering into the woods, I remembered that Winston Churchill called depression his black dog, a mercurial beast he tempered by painting sea- and land-scapes. Drinking is my black dog. I may wield my own charms of writing and knitting to temper that devil, but I would always be the woman who had burned her daughter's dolls. Nonetheless, when I quit drinking, I quit. Even on the hardest days of my divorce, I hadn't gone back.

Teeth chattering from the cold, I got back in my car, restarted the engine, and turned on to the highway. I headed up the mountain pass. I would survive another winter.

twelve

The Bullshit American Dream

With a cleaver, Molly diced a red onion. "He keeps messaging me, and I keep saying, 'Dude, uh-uh. No flipping way.'"

"You're sure that's a hard no?" Gabriela handed me a floury tortilla, and I laid the doughy round in a hot cast-iron skillet to fry.

"I'm positive. He's just too dumb to get it. Plus, he's dated every other girl in town, so he has to keep asking me."

"Even more reason to nix the invitation," I said. My phone chirruped. Glancing at the number, I handed Molly the tongs for the tortillas and said, "I'll go upstairs."

When I reached the second-floor landing, I pressed the green button. "Hello. Brett speaking." I stepped into my bedroom and closed the door behind me.

"This is Sam McDowell. I'm returning your message from this morning."

"Thanks for calling me back. Katie Whitaker gave me your number." The scent of lilacs from the blooming bush below my bedroom window drifted in on a gentle breeze. "I'm a librarian, and I'm looking for more information about substance abuse, specifically on how to maintain long-term sobriety. Katie said you might be willing to meet with me?"

"Absolutely. I'll share as much or as little you'd like."

We agreed to meet the following Sunday at the library.

Last fall, I had meant to call Sam after I met Katie at the diner, but then I had that tooth infection, and I was busy writing the library's annual report, and calling Sam slipped my mind. Then, after meeting with Chief Cochran and US Attorney Nolan, I began to feel that I'd gotten the upper hand on understanding addiction. I had an *I've got this* attitude. But that winter afternoon in my car when the desire to drink reemerged from my past with its old power, I knew my addiction was still with me. How could I live with the fear that addiction might overpower me again?

That very morning, as I put my foot on a shovel in my garden, digging a hole for a pea fence, I suddenly remembered what Christina Nolan said about how I needed to face what frightens me. So I called Sam, wanting to know more about what it was like for him, years into sobriety after abusing opioids.

Smoke from frying tortillas diffused upward through the open stairwell. I headed down the stairs, but paused when I heard Molly's voice.

"Let Mom figure out whatever this thing is."

"Why does she need to do this?" asked Gabriela.

"Who knows. But she does. Trust me."

∽

Sunday afternoon carried in the first wave of summer humidity. When I arrived at the library, I propped open the door with a rock, hoping for a breeze as the library has no air-conditioning. To keep the room cool, I kept the fluorescent lights off.

I was writing my monthly librarian report at the long table in the adult stacks when Sam walked in the door. He paused in the doorway, a shadowy figure against the sunlight streaming around him.

"Sam?" I stood up.

"You're Brett?" he asked, his voice deep. With short black hair and bushy eyebrows, he stepped farther into the room, blinking to adjust to the dimness. "I've never been to Woodbury before. It's so lush in that last narrow section, coming up the hill."

I closed my laptop and walked over to greet him. Wearing khaki shorts and a pressed button-down shirt, Sam looked the picture of business casual.

We shook hands. "That's the Woodbury pass. Driving those switchbacks can get dicey in the winter."

He looked around, a stainless steel water bottle in one hand. "This is a nice little library. It's just one room?"

"That other room, through that door over there, is technically the school's territory, although I use it for programs. School's the busiest time here. But during the summer and on some Saturdays, around here it can feel like it's just me and the turtles laying eggs in the ball field."

Sam looked over his shoulder out the door. "Really?"

"I've seen huge snappers lay eggs in the sandy stretch between second and third base. The kids know to keep their distance. They're not going anywhere near snapping turtles." I laughed, then gestured at the table and chairs. We sat down. "I appreciate you driving all the way out here."

"I grew up in Plattsburgh, right across the lake from Burlington, so I got to know that city really well, especially the college parties. But I've never been to this part of Vermont. These little rural towns are really interesting."

I laughed. "I doubt the kids around here would agree with that assessment."

"Point taken." He set the water bottle on the table between us. "You have questions about substance abuse and recovery?"

"Yes. Let me think where to begin . . . Well, in brief, shortly after I started working here, I realized the library had been broken into during the off hours, for years, by a local man who was rumored to be a heroin user. That made me start asking sharper questions about opioid use."

"Where's this man now?"

A hummingbird hovered in the doorway, wings whirring, then disappeared. "He committed suicide last year."

Sam winced. "That's unfortunate. How old was he?"

"Thirty-two."

"Only a few years older than me." Sam's wide eyebrows rose. "If you heard he was using, he probably was."

"I know. But after he died, I realized I had let the rumors scare me away from trying to help him. I began to wonder whether I might have acted differently if I had known more about opioid abuse, as opposed to acting from fear."

"You shouldn't blame yourself for his suicide."

"I don't, really. I didn't even know him, so to say I was responsible for his death is to put me at the center of something that's not my business. But it's more complicated than that. I'm a recovering alcoholic. Of all people, I should have treated this man better. Instead, I put all my energy into getting him arrested. I just wanted him out of the library and out of my way."

Sam uncapped his water bottle and took a draft. "The thing is, of course, hindsight can be 20/20."

"Right. Like that famous line from Kierkegaard. You know it? 'Life can only be understood backwards, but it must be lived forwards.' However, I have what my daughters might call a compulsion to learn something from his death. People who suffer from addiction are so covered with shame and stigma — and fear, I'm going to add that in, too, because this whole conversation is equally about the thousand faces of fear — that I realized if I didn't really get to the heart of what addiction is, then I could never open my heart with any amount of empathy."

"You said you met with others in recovery?"

I picked up my pen and turned it around and around in my hand. "I've spoken with a few people, who helped me see the connections between trauma and addiction. But Katie said you have a supportive and loving family. How did you end up using opioids?"

"You want me to just dive in? For obvious reasons, this is a subject I've thought a great deal about."

"Please."

"Okay," Sam began in his low voice, "so my parents are white-collar professionals, liberals with a *New Yorker* subscription and a meat share at the local farmers' market. I need to say at the very beginning that I love my parents and my two sisters. I know people often turn to substance abuse because of childhood trauma, but that wasn't true for me."

"Was a sports injury your introduction?"

"No. I wasn't much of an athlete. In high school, I was bored. The friends I hung out with liked to party. On weekends, we smoked pot and drank and did psychedelics. My parents weren't happy about it, but, at the time, I didn't care. My peers were my whole world. Then, one day, someone gave me a pill that changed my life."

"Really?" I asked. "You can do a drug once and fall in love with it?"

"The first time you take opioids it feels like you're surrounded by a warm, really soft blanket. That sounds like a cliché, but there isn't a way to describe the pleasure that you feel. Everything else was just gone."

"I haven't talked about this in years, but I smoked opium in college. That experience was exactly like you describe — everything was just gone."

The summer I was nineteen, I lived with my boyfriend, Duncan, in a cabin surrounded by woods near Marlboro College, not far from Brattleboro, Vermont. One day, we bought six marble-sized packages of opium wrapped in aluminum foil from another student. That night, Duncan dug at the black, sticky substance with his knife tip, and we smoked it from his stone pipe. The cabin was so far out in the woods that the one-room shack lacked both power and running water, so we lit the cabin at night with a single glass-globed kerosene lamp. Inhaling the opium, I felt as if my body were melting into the amber glow, blissfully peaceful.

The next morning, Duncan and I lay in bed, talking about those silver packets. In my memory, we were a little afraid of that drug's draw, and yet we were captivated. We agreed to ration the substance to once a week. That night, however, we smoked it again, transporting ourselves back to that radiant, otherworldly realm. The following night, we likely would have smoked again if the opium hadn't disappeared from our cabin. Duncan believed the student who had sold us the six packets had stolen our stash while we were at work.

"I hadn't thought of that opium in years. We didn't have access to more, as our source had dried up, but what if we had? My life, or my boyfriend's life, might have been completely different."

"It's an interesting speculation. A lot of people assume addiction always has sinister roots, like childhood trauma, mental illness, or overprescribed opioids after a surgery or injury. But when I started, drugs were just fun for me. That's what's so scary about opioids — it's so easy to start using, but nearly impossible to stop."

"Maybe this is partly what bothers me so much. I mean, I get the obvious connection between addiction and trauma, and the maybe not-so-obvious connection between addiction and material and spiritual poverty. But on another level, I wonder how much of our life is just random. How did you get from smoking weed to using heroin? Isn't that a huge leap?"

"It's not a leap, it's a drift. All through high school, I held to this moral line that I would never do heroin. By the time I started at Johnson State, I was using a lot of pills. At that time — about ten years ago — pills were everywhere. Everyone's mother or grandmother had a prescription. When those prescriptions started tightening up, pills got harder to find and way more expensive. You couldn't just open anyone's medicine cabinet anymore and help yourself. Black-market heroin started flooding in, because the demand for drugs hadn't disappeared. Honestly, when I first tried heroin, I was probably hanging out with someone who used it, and it was probably two in the morning. I can't remember."

In his third year at Johnson, Sam was busted for smoking pot. College staff searched his dorm room and confiscated ninety morphine pills Sam had intended to sell. To avoid expulsion, Sam withdrew from the school, but it was so late in the semester that he received zeros on his permanent record — a consequence that didn't bother him at the time.

"Did your parents know what was going on?"

"They must have suspected, but, like any user, I was very adept at deception."

"That's part of the terrain, isn't it? I lied for years about how much and when I'd been drinking." I stacked my papers and pen on my laptop and pushed it to the end of the table. "So when you left Johnson, how did you support yourself? Your drug habit must have been expensive."

"No kidding. Like, around two hundred dollars a day. I couldn't make that kind of money with some kind of shit job, so I started dealing. If you're buying drugs, other people often ask you to pick up something for them. So you add on a few bucks, and you've provided for yourself for the day. Most low-level dealers aren't out to make bank; they're just feeding their own habits."

Every week for about half a year, Sam drove to Albany, New York, and boarded the train to New York City. "In the city, I would see an acquaintance for maybe twenty minutes, get what I wanted, and immediately take the train back to Albany. Once, we had to meet his people later that night or the next day, so I stayed overnight at his house. He still lived with his parents, and he had told them I was a friend who had an interview in the city early the next day for a music internship. It was the most surreal conversation. I didn't know anything about music and, fortunately, they didn't, either. I just bull-shitted my way through."

"That's just weird."

"Everything about dealing is weird."

"What's it like to deal?"

"Well . . . I'll try to sketch it out. First, heroin's sold in small glass-ine bags used by stamp collectors about this size." Sam raised one hand, thumb and finger about an inch apart. "I used to pay between thirty and forty dollars per bag."

"What year was this?"

He thought for a moment. "Around 2012? That period is a little foggy for me. Anyway, each of those little bags held a tenth of a gram, but I suspected it was often a lot less, sometimes half that amount. The bags were folded over and taped shut — probably someone's day job in the city. If you think about it, so many people are involved in this story. I was just a tiny cog."

"Drugs are a business, too, just an underground one."

"That's for sure. When I started dealing, I quickly realized why so many people sell drugs: you can make a lot of money. In New York City, I could buy a bundle of heroin — that's ten glassine bags — for forty dollars, then take it back to Vermont and resell that bundle for two hundred. Often, I'd buy several bundles at a time. I was at the bottom tier of a complicated system, but the math should have worked in my favor. I consumed every bit of that profit, though."

"Who were your customers?"

"At first, just people I knew, but soon that changed, too. I'd sell to anyone who had cash. I drove between Plattsburgh, Burlington, and Johnson, spending a couple of nights every week in each town. In addition to heroin, I was also fronted cocaine, which raised the stakes even higher, since I had to sell it to repay the debt. I spent a lot of time driving and on the phone. In a strange way, I felt busy and important, like I was getting stuff done. For a little while, I was really into the coolness of the scene, but in the back of my mind, I was always worried about getting caught."

I pulled my knitting needles and yarn out of my backpack and set them in my lap. The next step was joining the unfinished sleeves into the yoke. "It's hard for me to picture a life like that. I think the worry would have killed me."

"I was incredibly anxious the entire time. Hardly anyone talks about this, but when you're using, life appears very straightforward, because it's organized around a single goal: getting high. It's like this: You spend all your money today to get drugs. You know there's no more in your bank account, and the rent is due Friday. But you blow it anyway. You figure you'll get more money tomorrow. But tomorrow's money doesn't pay the rent. You figure out the rent the day the rent is due."

"Your thinking was that shortsighted? Down to the day?"

"Definitely. You tell yourself you're free, that you're living life the way you want, but you're completely beholden to the drugs."

"When I spoke with our local police chief, he compared drug addiction to a zombie apocalypse. People who are heavily involved with abusing substances are in a different world."

"That's an apt comparison."

Through the open door, I watched a fat bumblebee fly by in a zigzagging wobble. I had my own tally of broken promises about when I would quit drinking — tomorrow, or after this last bottle of wine, or next week. "How did you break that cycle, Sam? Did you ask for help? Maybe from your parents?"

"No. Like so many people, I believed I should be able to pull myself up by my bootstraps. That I got myself into this mess, and I should be able to get myself out. Also, I didn't really want anyone to know."

"Oh, how I understand that."

For a moment, we contemplated each other's gaze. "What happened, Sam?"

"I got lucky. That's what happened." A friend told Sam he had heard from a relative that New York law enforcement had connected Sam's name with dealing. "I panicked. I was terrified about getting arrested and charged with multiple felonies, so I stopped everything that very day. I began self-medicating with street Suboxone, to hold off withdrawal, which absolutely sucked. But black-market Suboxone is hard to find, and sometimes I couldn't get it. Or I'd have to drive all over to buy it. I quit dealing and got a job, because I thought that would look better if I did get arrested. Eventually, I wrote my parents a long confessional email. Their response was very loving — really, one of the biggest reliefs of my life — and I enrolled in a MAT program using their insurance."

"How did MAT go for you? I've heard grumbling about that program. Some people say it swaps one addiction for another, or that it's too easy."

He shook his head. "Anyone who says that doesn't understand how difficult addiction is. My body and my life were consumed by the need for drugs. From the moment I woke up in the morning, I was focused on where that next high was going to come from. To get better, I had to physically detox from drugs, but I also had to redefine my life. The MAT program gave me the space for my body to regain health. I also had to attend group counseling sessions that I mostly thought were bullshit. People lied just to get through them. MAT isn't a perfect program, by any means. But I also had daily drug tests. Passing those kept me motivated to move through the program so I wouldn't have to show up every day. Every part was incredibly challenging. I don't think I could have done it without the Suboxone. Before that, I had tried maybe twenty times to quit using." He pushed his chair back slightly. "What was getting sober like for you?"

"Different. I was fortunate enough that I never experienced that level of addiction. I've seen DTs,* and I know what that looks like. I never approached that level of addiction. I never got up in the morning and drank. But that doesn't mean I wouldn't have gotten there."

"Did you check into rehab?"

The day's humidity fattened, cloying where my hair hung down my neck. "I never did any kind of rehab. I actually chanced across a book about habits and realized that, for me, drinking was a nightly habit I could learn to change. Every morning, I told myself not drinking was the one thing I was going to accomplish that day. It was really hard — exactly as you said. But it did get easier as I hit one week, then one month, then six months, then a year. Now it seems forever since I reiterated that goal every morning. In the beginning, though, it took every shred of my strength to overcome that desire for drink. This might sound strange, but I actually substituted knitting for drinking. It kept my hands moving and fed my hunger for creativity. Over time, I've become pretty good at it."

---

*Alcohol withdrawal can cause delirium tremens. Symptoms include severe shivering, increased heart rate, and hallucinations.

"Anyone who's gotten sober, if it's just for a little while, has a story of what worked for them." Sam lifted up his silver water bottle. "Is there somewhere I could refill this?"

"Of course. There's a sink in the other room."

I walked over to my desk and picked up a stack of novels. One of my patrons, Krystal, read voraciously, but her returned books always smelled of cigarettes and required an airing. I stepped outside and leaned the novels against the wooden garden bed. Bending over, I picked a dandelion and cradled the bright yellow blossom in my hand, like a miniature shining sun. When Molly was in preschool, she would greet me with fat handfuls of dandelion bouquets when I picked her up. I nestled the blossom in a toy frying pan a child had left, full with black dirt, on the grass. How much I had wanted to be a better mother.

Blinking away tears, I walked back in the library, where Sam was waiting at the table.

I sat down across from him. "Where were we?"

∽

"Sometimes," Sam said, his voice raspy with phlegm, "I wonder, would I have gotten clean if I hadn't been threatened with prison?" He cleared his throat with a cough. "I like to think so, that one day I would've hit rock bottom hard enough, but I don't know that for sure. The drugs are so strong. I've seen a lot of people who desperately wanted to get clean but couldn't. At that level of opioid addiction, there's really only three outcomes — get clean, go to prison, or die. In the end, so much of my story is just plain luck."

"Luck's a funny thing, though." With my finger, I prodded the gold ball of yarn. "You have to be open to it, too. The day I quit drinking, the same thousand reasons I should have quit were there the day before, and the day before that, too. For me, addiction was a fog I lived in for years. I wanted sobriety for a very long time. Then, one day, I saw the chance to get out. I'm wondering if it was the same way for you — was that phone call the arrow that split the fog?"

A quiet voice called, "Hello?" A young woman and a small girl wearing a cotton-candy-pink dress with purple polka dots stood in the library's open doorway.

"I'm sorry," I said. "I'm not actually open."

"Could we look at that box of free books over there? I see some for kids."

Sam turned around and said, "Please, take your time."

"Take as many as you'd like," I added. "There are some really nice picture books in the back."

While we waited, I asked Sam, "Do you have kids yourself?"

"No. My partner and I are not in any rush to start a family. What I'm considering now is graduate school. That's a big impetus to get off my Suboxone script, because I don't want that to follow me."

"What are you interested in studying?"

"I haven't completely decided. I'm interested in social justice, incarceration, and also drug rehabilitation, but I'm not sure if I want that subject to dominate my life. I'm also fascinated by stigma and how it affects our behavior."

Finished picking through the box, the mother and her daughter meandered away into the sunny afternoon.

When they stepped out, Sam said, "Going back to the factor of luck? I've thought a lot about how the randomness of the life we're born into affects our lives. As a white man from an affluent background, I know I have advantages that other people don't, such as parents who paid for my treatment. I acknowledge I was a criminal, and I own that completely. Don't get me wrong. Yet I'm also really aware that I probably had a different outcome, at least in part, not because of my own doing, but because of my privileged position. But if I had gone to prison, would I have come out of it a better citizen? I don't think so."

I spread the half-finished sweater on the table and smoothed it out. "I worry I hide behind my own privilege, too. My addiction was awful for me and my family, but it could have been so much worse. I never had to go to rehab, was never publicly shamed, and didn't have legal or health problems." The yellow ball of yarn rolled off the table. I bent down and rewound it. "But when I became a single mother, things got iffy very quickly. I struggled with money. My ex-husband kept breaking into our house. After I was twice refused a restraining order, I finally went to a women's shelter and begged for help. Before that, I'd never worried before about where the next meal for my kids was coming from, or frequented food shelves, or relied on public assistance. All my life, I'd benefited from privilege, and I'd never realized it."

"That's the definition of privilege, isn't it? It's there, and we use it, but don't acknowledge it, or even see it?"

"I think that's exactly right. This journey of asking questions about addiction in my own community made me see the connection between addiction and trauma and how profoundly poverty shapes lives. But I also began to realize we often don't understand our circumstances, at least at the time. So much of our life seems simply the roll of the circumstantial dice." Fleetingly, I wondered how different Shauna's life might have been had she been the daughter of, say, an anesthesiologist.

Beneath those bushy eyebrows, Sam studied me.

I continued, "But as I'm listening to you, I keep wondering if there was something deeper in your story. As you've said over and over, addiction is complex, but sobriety is, too. I understand why you don't want fear of jail to get the credit for why you got sober. But were there factors besides fear of prison that made you stick with getting clean?"

With his wrist, Sam wiped sweat from his brow. "It wasn't like a light switch turned on. I knew I wanted to stop using drugs long before I actually did. I'd tried maybe twenty times to get clean." He glanced out the open door. "When I heard I might be charged with multiple felonies, I was so afraid I didn't even travel back into New York State for over a year." Golden-flecked pollen blew by with a slow breeze. "But the thing is, I wouldn't have been as worried about going to prison if my parents wouldn't have had to experience it as well. Even when I argued with my dad, which happened a lot, I always admired him. What if it was just me and a mom who didn't really care, and a dad who's maybe in jail or not around? I didn't care if I felt bad, but I definitely did not want my parents to suffer. Even at my worst, I never wanted to let them down. I hadn't realized this before, but that's probably why I got better."

In the grass outside the library door, a lone cricket chirped. Sam's story reminded me of that famous line from Rumi: "The wound is the place where light enters." Of all the wounds in my life, those few sentences from my daughters cut the hardest. But their words carved a space for their love to stream in, lighting my way back to them.

༄

"What are your parents like, Sam?"

"My mother's a Buddhist."

"That explains your thoughtfulness."

"My father should get credit, too. His older brother had mental health issues that were exacerbated by substance abuse. He died fairly young, and his death was assumed a suicide. My sisters and I knew about this uncle, but no one really spoke about him. Now I realize my father's experience with his brother shaped the way he responded to me. My father wasn't just going to throw money at me, because he already knew sobriety requires more than resources. I'm not going to belittle the importance of money, but it's not enough. I think this goes back to what makes this problem so difficult. Sobriety isn't as simple as getting clean. It's what you do afterward, and how you rebuild your life. It can be very hard to maintain any type of sobriety if you don't have guidance about how to stay sober." Sam scraped off a hardened smear of glue on the tabletop with his thumbnail.

"What keeps you sober? The Suboxone?"

"Suboxone was, and still is, an enormous part of my recovery. I also cut myself off from everyone I used to hang out with and started a whole new life. I kept working and reenrolled in school. But I'm still isolated, and I don't often talk about my past. How can I tell anyone I once ran drugs from New York to Vermont?"

Despite the seriousness of the conversation, I laughed. "I can imagine the dissonance."

"Yeah. It's not like I ever worked that into idle conversation. When I started getting clean, I went back and apologized to some people I had hurt with my actions, like a counselor at Johnson I'd lied to. But other people I drifted away from. Sometimes, as hardhearted as this sounds, you have to move on. By the time I reenrolled in college, the people I had known before had all left or graduated, which gave me a chance to restart." He stood up and glanced around the library. "I guess it's getting late."

I stood up, too, and reached across the table to shake his hand. "I really appreciated talking with you today," I said. "I never joined a sobriety group. It was only when I began doing this research that I actually started talking to people about my own experiences."

"You're a member of this dubious club, too."

We wandered out the door, walking past the red-painted, two-story schoolhouse with large, multipaned windows to the empty playground, where I picked up a tiny orange sweatshirt a child had dropped. In the nearby forest, sparrows chattered and robins chirruped. Spring is the mating and nest-building season.

"Sam," I asked, "how do you live with knowing that relapse, that slipping back into that kind of life, is possible? I realized this winter that recovery has no end, but goes on and on. I don't mean that trite old phrase 'once an alcoholic, always an alcoholic,' but lasting recovery requires digging deeper with time. First, I had to quit drinking — and that was a bitch, really — and then I had to figure out my life. Get a different job. Walk out of a terrible marriage. Eventually sell our house and move to another town. Everything that spun my life and my daughters' lives in a healthier direction came out of my sobriety." I shook out the sweatshirt, scattering wood shavings and dirt. "But then, when a man died after leaving this library, I forced myself to face the truth that I had never really acknowledged my addiction. If I had, I might have had more compassion for him. I might have realized that he and I, like you and I —" I stretched out my hand with that little sweatshirt to Sam. "We're alike."

"Recovery is a journey for a lifetime. Only a fool would think relapse couldn't happen to them. When I first went back to Johnson, the past seemed to have vanished. No one knew who I was when I was using. Then, I was a drop-out. Now I'm heading toward a PhD program. In that way, I'm a completely different kind of student, but my past made me, and it will make my future, too. I'm here, talking with you, because I got lucky — damn lucky — and I know it. I didn't go to jail. I didn't overdose and die. I got sober." He gazed across the field, at the place where the rusty chain-link fence parted. There a mown path led into a narrow parting in the dense woods. "In a way, it's comforting to know that you don't have to be a product of your environment. Wherever your story starts, it doesn't have to finish there. If addiction runs in your family, as it does in mine, it doesn't have to be a death wish."

Sam's fist white-knuckled that silver water bottle. "Here's what I learned the hard way: Be determined. Have accountability to yourself. Be conscious and self-aware regarding your actions. And take help, even if you feel you don't deserve it. It was very hard for me to accept help, because I felt bad about the things I had done to other people. Why should I get better when I had done these terrible things for so long? I had always believed in the self-made man, that bullshit 'American dream' of make your own life. But eventually, I had to accept help or I wasn't going to get better. It's never all up to you. That's impossible."

Impossible? I folded the tiny sweatshirt and held it in one hand. "It's interesting to hear you say that, because I always considered drinking my weakness, my failing, and my problem to solve alone. I was so ashamed that I never considered asking for help, even when I desperately needed it, and it would have made all the difference for my family. And while my addiction was mine — I was driving that train, as you said — the roots of my addiction spread far beyond my life. When I think about it, even though I always told myself I got better on my own, that isn't really true. Without my daughters, I wouldn't have cared at all. They were the only reason I came back."

A small cloud passed between us and the sun, dropping its shadow, then scudded away in a breeze. I blinked in the sudden, bright light.

Sam squinted and cupped his eyes with one hand. "The kicker is, no one can tell you that when you're in the thick of addiction. There's no magic formula out. Take all the help anyone offers; that's my advice. Because in the end, you have to get yourself out."

I walked beside him as he headed to the parking lot. "Somehow we believe in magic, though, don't we? I don't know if this is a uniquely American phenomenon or a human one, but we so often seem to believe that happiness is a place where we'll eventually arrive, like achieving the American Dream. But I'm thinking now the world doesn't work that way. Here, I've been sober for years. But my marriage ended like a train wreck. When I finally worked up the nerve to get sober, I realized that fog of addiction had hidden my husband's unraveling mental health for years. In so many ways, my life and my daughters' lives have gotten immeasurably better, but there's been nothing easy about any of this. And I can't help but worry about my daughters. They come from a family where addiction runs hard and furious, and where mental illness imprints on their genes, too."

We stood in the schoolhouse's cool shadow.

"Brett, life is messy. Sometimes terrifying. But your daughters aren't alone, either. They have you, for starters."

Tears suddenly blinded my vision. Blinking rapidly, I looked upward, wiping my face with my fingers. "This schoolhouse is on the historic registry. It's a beauty, isn't it? Tin ceilings, mahogany woodwork. Built back when schools were the town's pride."

Sam stepped back and appraised the building. "How many students go here?"

"Kindergarten through sixth grade? Less than fifty now, but it was designed for eighty to a hundred students."

"Fifty kids total? Wow." Sam surveyed the landscape: the playground, the raised garden beds dotted with cucumber seedlings, the dandelion-studded ball field flanked by woods. "What's the dating scene like when the kids get to high school?"

"I'm sure a few find true love. For others, it's a real challenge."

He looked at me and smiled. I suddenly realized I hadn't yet seen him smile. "A real challenge could be the theme of our conversation today. And yet here we both are, on a beautiful Sunday afternoon. Enjoy what's left of it." He waved good-bye, then hurried around the building and out of sight.

thirteen

A Field of Yellow Flowers

Over our Caesar salads at the diner last fall, Katie Whitaker had also urged me to speak with Dawn and Greg Tatro, who lost their daughter, Jenna Rae Tatro, to an overdose six months before, in February. At twenty-six, Jenna had been only a few years older than Molly. But months passed, and I didn't reach out to the Tatros. At first, I told myself it was because I didn't want to intrude on their grief. But the truth is that I was afraid. To lose a child to an overdose seemed the very worst outcome of addiction.

Then the Tatros made the local news when they purchased the empty St. John the Apostle Church in Johnson. They planned to convert the property into a recovery center. So the couple was on my mind when, shortly after my conversation with Sam, I woke before dawn and lay in bed listening to a summer rain pitter-pattering on the leaves of the enormous mock orange bush beneath my open window. I had come this far, I thought.

I got up and made coffee, then opened my laptop and emailed the Tatros.

Almost immediately, Dawn wrote back with her phone number and asked me to call.

"Hello," I said when she answered. "I'm Brett."

"Thanks for asking about what we're doing. You said you're a librarian?"

"I am. I know this is a lot to ask, but I'm looking for more information about what you and your husband are doing to support people in recovery from addiction. I wondered if one or both of you might have time to talk."

"We'd be glad to. Don't worry; your request isn't unusual. But would you mind coming to our house? We run a construction business, and summer is our busiest season."

We agreed to meet the following Monday morning, also Gabriela's first day as a junior counselor at my friend Heather's art camp. When she was a wispy-haired three-year-old, Gabriela had joined her first clay class at Heather's studio, sitting on a stool with apron strings wound twice around her tiny waist and bow-tied in front. She was so small that Heather lifted her onto the stool. Gabriela and Lucia — girls who had known each other since they were babes in arms — had anticipated this grown-up position for months.

✍

Monday morning, Gabriela and I met Lucia and her mother, Jessica, at a turnout along the Lamoille River, where graveled Kate Brook Road joins Route 15. Clasping her backpack, Gabriela hurried from my car to the backseat of Jessica's bright-blue Subaru, buckled the seat belt, and bent forward to talk with Lucia in the passenger seat.

I unbuckled, too, and walked over to the driver's-side window. "Thanks," I told Jessica. "I'll meet you here at three. And I'll do the driving tomorrow."

"No problem. Have a nice day." Jessica drove to the stop sign, then turned and disappeared around a hillside. Standing on the side of the dirt road, I watched as the dust kicked up by her tires slowly settled, then gazed down the steep bank at the shallow, rock-studded river, its glassy surface sprinkled with pollen and dust. A lone brown-feathered duck bobbed along the current.

Our old house was three miles up Kate Brook Road. Where I stood, the dirt road cut between two large fields, planted intermittently with potatoes, hay, or industrial hemp. Every school day for five years, I met my friend Heather at this turnout to carpool our girls to a Waldorf school half an hour's drive down Route 14. I usually picked up Heather's daughters, Ruby and Cora, and drove the morning leg. Some afternoons, I arrived at this turnout early for pickup. If Gabriela, who was a baby, had fallen asleep, I would unroll the windows and let her nap. In those quiet moments, I leaned against our old blue Volvo, watching clouds sweep across the sky.

On warm afternoons, Heather and I often dawdled at the turnout, talking while our daughters played under the wild apple trees along the roadside. The girls had created an imaginary realm, with a shifting storyline involving a missing mother and wily children. Come late May and early June, the four girls loved to leap across the tops of hay bales.

That Monday morning, with a few spare minutes before I needed to be on my way to the Tatros, I walked along the riverbank. At a swath of long-stemmed rudbeckia, I paused and picked a bouquet, remembering Seth Hubbell, a man who had written a short memoir about farming as a colonist in this valley. In February 1789, not far down the river from that turnout, Hubbell packed a snowshoe trail into the Vermont woods with his wife and five daughters. For tools, he carried one ax and an old hoe. Growing faint from hard labor and hunger, he sometimes caught a fish from the river and roasted its unsalted flesh over a fire, devouring the creature steaming hot with his fingers. I imagined him kneeling on banks of the flowing river, teeming with aquatic life, the soil around him harrowed open to the sky, exposing fat grubs and scurrying ants, the soil's dampness quickly drying in the breeze sweeping down the river valley. Hubbell contemplated a sky never crossed by contrails, gazing up at great migratory sweeps of geese and passenger pigeons, now long since extinct. During his early years farming this land, Hubbell buried his first wife and a daughter; at the end of his long life, he counted with satisfaction his progeny of seventy-six souls. Like so many others, I had an idyllic notion that the world was greener and lovelier in another place or time. But while rhapsodizing about Hubbell farming this fertile piece of earth was easy, I knew such dreaming was indulgent. The wolves of hunger clamored at Hubbell's door.

I wandered back to my car and paused for a moment before I opened the door. I scanned the strip of green field and the empty dirt road. Twenty-five years ago that summer, Eric and I had bought that hunting camp and eight acres up the road. I no longer even knew where he was. Rumors circulated that he'd wandered off to protest the North Dakota pipeline. As the morning grew hotter, I stood there remembering the final time we'd met at this roadside turnout. In those days, we were still married, trying to figure out which way our lives would turn. Three miles down the road from our house, out of our daughters' curious ears, we sat in his truck, arguing. I leaned my forehead against the cool glass of the passenger window, thinking about our daughters, home alone, who would be wondering about dinner. Three coyotes trotted by in the field and disappeared over the riverbank. Eric kept talking and talking. I unrolled the window and listened to the coyotes yipping as dusk swallowed up the remaining daylight.

∽

The stretch of Route 15 from Hardwick to Johnson passes along riverside fields cleared during Hubbell's time, still cultivated today with corn and hay. Interspersed among farms are car dealerships, gas stations, pharmacies, two-hundred-year-old farmhouses, and mobile homes. Approaching Johnson from the east, the highway descends abruptly into switchbacks. There tight mountainsides shrink the light until the pass empties into the village and opens up into a handful of streets. The campus of Northern Vermont University — recently renamed after Johnson State College, Sam McDowell's alma mater, merged with Lyndon State College — sprawls across a hillside above the elementary school. Located at the confluence of the Lamoille and Gihon Rivers, the town is prone to flooding, its valley climate slightly more temperate than Hardwick's. Daffodils bloom earlier here.

On the other side of Johnson, I turned off Route 15 and wound up a dirt road past a horse barn to the Tatros' house. Dawn answered the door. I crouched down and unstrapped my dusty sandals, leaving them beside the door.

In her sunny, high-ceilinged kitchen, Dawn, tanned and fit, hurried around, wiping down the counters. "Coffee? Tea? I didn't know what you'd want."

I shook my head. "I'm fine, thanks."

"Greg so wanted to meet you, but he was called into a meeting at the last minute."

She dried her hands on a dish towel, then gestured to a large framed photo of a pretty young woman displayed on an easel against the wall. "This is Jenna," Dawn said, her eyes teary. "I wish she was here to meet you."

"She looks so much like you."

Dawn led me into their living room, where I sat on a wide leather couch. The room was designed for entertaining, with comfortable furniture and a polished wooden bar with a rack of wineglasses hung overhead. Dawn stood at the bar, rifling through a basket overflowing with mail. "We get letters from all over the country. Some are from people we know, but many are from strangers sending condolence cards or sharing their own stories. They're so powerful that we only read a few a day." She sat beside me on the couch and spread out photographs of different sizes on the coffee table. "I wanted to show you these, so you could get a better picture of Jenna."

Dawn told me that Jenna and her best friend traveled around the world during a gap year after high school, visiting India and Dubai. "Jenna always wanted to experience new things. She lived on the edge, but she was such a good girl. She brought strays home all the time — lost cats and dogs, an owl. Once a homeless woman. 'Jenna . . .' I said, but she told me if we could help others, then we should."

When she returned from her travels, Jenna enrolled in Johnson State College. At the end of her first semester, on Christmas Eve, Jenna's boyfriend beat her up so badly that she visited the emergency room. "She had a broken heart and bruises, but no cracked bones or serious physical injuries. The doctor wrote her a thirty-day prescription for OxyContin, with a refill. He told her to take the medication as often as needed. So she did. That's how this started."

"On the phone," I said, "you mentioned that she struggled with addiction for six years? That's a long time."

"Of course, we didn't realize at the beginning that we had six years of this ahead of us. When Jenna came home from the hospital, she was depressed and didn't get out of bed. She and the boyfriend had broken up, but he kept bugging her, and that made her miserable. She never went back to school, which made her more unhappy. On top of all that, when she didn't take drugs, she was dopesick." Dawn closed her eyes for a moment, then opened them again. "When she told me she was using heroin, I was like, Jenna — heroin? I was terrified."

Desperate for help, Dawn attended meetings at the nearby recovery center, where Meg Goulet now works. As prominent business owners, neither she nor Greg was keen to speak publicly about their family's struggles. "I was so ashamed when I walked in that meeting and admitted my daughter was a heroin addict. But you know what? Those people were just like me. We were all struggling."

"In my experience, people have reason to hide their addiction. There's such a harsh judgment levied against anyone who struggles with an addiction."

"And against that person's family." Dawn crossed her knees tightly and folded her arms over her chest, leaning back into the couch, away from me. "One thing I've learned is that we can't begin to address this problem if we insist on hiding it. That's partly why I talk with anyone who asks, like you today. Education is huge. It would have helped us so much. Six years ago, I didn't understand so many things." She stood up, grabbed a tissue from a box on the bar, and wiped her eyes. "We train horses. Maybe you saw them down by the road?"

"I wondered if they were yours."

Dawn sat down beside me again, clutching that crumpled, damp Kleenex in her hand. "I told her, 'Jenna, don't be like the two-year-old horses we trained, the ones who lie down when hitched to a cart and refuse to pull. The horses with fire in their hearts succeed. Be that horse,' I urged her. 'Have fire in your heart.' I really believed she could get herself out. But Jenna kept insisting that her addiction was so much bigger than herself, that the cravings were out of this world. In the beginning, I didn't know how true that was. Then our lives got crazier and crazier."

"Crazy and addiction always seem to go hand in hand."

Dawn shook her head. "I don't mean just partying or staying out all night."

"What do you mean?"

"Here's a story of what our lives were like."

Jenna had been out of contact for days when Dawn got a call around two in the morning. "She was at a gas station, the one near the rotary on this side of Morrisville, and asked me to drive out and get her."

"I know the place."

"When I pulled up, she was wearing a little white skirt, covered with mud, and had black mascara streaks running down her face. 'What the hell?' I said. 'Who did this to you?' She said she had been dumped out of a car in the ditch along the road."

Using Jenna's directions and some guesswork, Dawn drove to a nearby mobile home park. "I was so pissed. I saw three people walking into a trailer with boarded-up windows, carrying groceries at three in the morning, and, bingo, I knew that had to be them." Leaving Jenna nodding off in the car, Dawn entered the trailer without knocking. The occupants insisted they didn't know Jenna, but when Dawn spied Jenna's purse in the room, she began arguing with one of the women. As the quarrel escalated, the woman grabbed the purse and banged it on Dawn's head.

Grimacing, Dawn snapped her fingers. "I told her, 'You're gonna fucking die.' I had no fear. I could lose it on this girl. I was so angry at her for doing this to my daughter. For throwing my daughter in a ditch. Like garbage." Suddenly, she said, Jenna appeared in the trailer, swaying unsteadily and babbling incoherently. "If it was just me, it's one thing, but I had to protect Jenna, which meant getting the hell out of there."

The strangers followed the Tatros outside and climbed all over Dawn's car, shouting through the windows, "You're crazy, you're crazy . . ."

"My God."

"That was one night."

⁊

"Jenna must have tried rehab?"

Dawn rolled her eyes. "Probably twenty times she cycled through places, all over the country." She ticked off locations on her fingers. "Texas, Arizona, multiple places in California, Massachusetts, Pennsylvania, Florida . . . Her last stay was in New Hampshire."

"Were any programs successful?"

"No. Jenna tried over and over to get sober, but every time she got close, she ran away. Once she started getting clean, she would begin to feel things again, and she couldn't bear that. She had such remorse for what she had done to people when she was using. I mean" — she lowered her voice — "Jenna stole from her grandmother; she didn't want to experience that again."

"I know what that's like." When I met Dawn's eyes, I saw she was looking at me attentively. "I'm an alcoholic in recovery."

"I see. Did you use opioids, too?"

"No. Though I've struggled, I've been fortunate in many ways. But after a suicide in my town, I realized that, even though I've been sober for years, I still feared addiction. My fear and ignorance led me to do things I shouldn't have done. I don't want to be voyeuristic, but I'm here because I want to understand addiction more deeply."

"Addiction is terrifying." Dawn began tapping her phone screen. "I'm going to give you a piece of the story I don't think you're expecting. Here's the thing: hardly anyone talks about the connection between drugs and gangs in Vermont." She held her phone between us and played a video of a scrawny, smiling man singing along to rap music. "He's responsible for Jenna's death. Watch here. See what he's pulling from his pocket." She pointed to a wad of cash about three inches thick in the man's hand. A large man loomed behind him. "That's his bodyguard."

"Where did you get this?"

"Facebook. It was posted the day after Jenna died."

"What's he singing? I can't make out the lines."

"Laugh at me. Laugh at me. Drugs, money, guns."

"What are you saying? Hold on. How is this man responsible for Jenna's death?"

Dawn turned off her phone and placed it screen-down on the table. "Jenna got tied up with a gang from Springfield, Massachusetts."

"Where would she even meet someone from a gang?"

"Through drugs. By the time the refills of that first prescription ran out, Jenna was addicted, and so she had to search for another source. Buying drugs brought her to the gang. She was such a pretty girl, and they bought her new clothes and gave her all the drugs she wanted. But they weren't giving her these things because they liked her. She was running drugs for them. She owed the gang so much money that they owned her."

Early one morning, Dawn drove to the apartment where her daughter was living, after Jenna called and revealed that she had guests who wouldn't leave. When Dawn arrived, she found four cars with out-of-state plates parked in the driveway. In one, a man dozed with his head on the steering wheel. "I used my key and walked in there. Four guys were on her couch and there was drug paraphernalia everywhere. Like a bull in a china cabinet, I ordered them to leave. Jenna said, 'Mom what are you doing here? Mom, you have to go.'" When the men refused to leave, Dawn left and phoned the police. "I said, I have the four biggest fricking dealers here, and the drugs are right on the table."

The officer asked if her daughter had a toothbrush in the apartment. "I was like, what does that have to do with anything?" Dawn discovered that her daughter's occupancy in the apartment, proved by the toothbrush, meant law enforcement needed a search warrant to enter, even though Dawn owned the apartment and she had made the request.

While Dawn was on the phone, the men disappeared. "Jenna called me and said, 'Thank you, Mom, but please, please, don't ever do that again.'"

"Why do you think she said that? Was she trying to protect you?"

"I don't know. Jenna often lied to me. Afterward, I began to piece things together. I think those men used the apartment as a distribution hub. They would set up shop Thursday night and stay until Sunday, when they went back to Massachusetts. Nobody thinks that would happen in a little town like this. People don't realize what's going on right under our noses."

"Did Jenna have a job? I'm trying to imagine what her daily life was like."

"You don't understand. Jenna couldn't hold a job. Using was her life. That's all she did."

"Her addiction was that severe?"

"Oh, yes. It had gotten to the point last December where she told me, 'I can't live like this anymore. I just pray every day that I'm going to die. I've done so many things, Mom, so many things I can't even tell you. When I start coming clean, I start feeling this stuff, and I can't bear it. I just want to start using again to numb.'"

"That must have been awful."

"But it wasn't just her addiction Jenna had to fight against. She was desperate to leave the gang, but that began to seem impossible, too. She was running drugs and was useful to them, but she knew everything, too, from dealers to drug houses. They didn't want to let her go. She couldn't turn to the police, because she was afraid of getting criminal charges herself. So she 'worked out' a deal where some other girl would run the gang's drugs."

"And take her place?"

"Yes. So she could get out." Dawn's phone buzzed; she powered it off. "This winter, while Jenna was in a rehab center in New Hampshire, Greg and I were in Costa Rica, working. Someone from the center's staff called one night and said word was circulating that Jenna was planning to leave. We didn't fly back, because she was twenty-six and an adult; she had checked herself out of numerous rehabs before. What could we have done? We didn't hear anything until three days later, when Jenna called us in Costa Rica. She'd had a vivid dream. Greg and I are Catholic, but Jenna wasn't. She had always insisted, 'That's not me, Mom.' But in this dream she had relived her addicted life — being homeless, not having enough food, without friends or a steady place to sleep, getting robbed, running from the law." Dawn pulled the bunched Kleenex from her pocket and wiped tears from her cheek. "She realized the pain of getting sober couldn't be worse than how she was living."

"This was all in a dream?"

"I know it might seem unbelievable that anyone could change so much just from a dream. Maybe you're thinking that Jenna was lying to us again. But the staff at the facility called us and said Jenna had turned a 180; she'd had a huge revelation. I really believed that this time she was going to stick with it."

"I don't have any difficulty believing that. When I was open and ready, a few words from my daughters changed me. I'm guessing Jenna reached that point."

During the next few weeks, Jenna worked through the recovery program, progressing to sober living in a shared apartment where she began transitioning from rehab back into the community. When she was about to receive her sixty-day sober chip, she called her parents and said she wanted to wait to accept it until they returned from Costa Rica. Shortly after that call, the center staff again phoned the Tatros. Jenna hadn't returned from a meeting. "I'm like, 'What do you mean? I just talked to her. She was so happy and excited about us coming home and meeting her friends.'"

When Dawn reached her daughter via text, Jenna told her mother she had made a terrible mistake.

Dawn pressed her hands over her abdomen. "I felt sick. I was like, 'What did you do, Jenna?'" Over text, Jenna explained. On her way from the sober house to a meeting, an acquaintance from the gang drove up and asked her to get in the car, "just to talk." Jenna did, and he drove away. He wouldn't let her out, she texted, so she was planning to run when he stopped. Would Dawn get her an Uber or taxi? "Absolutely," Dawn wrote back.

"But he didn't stop. Jenna kept apologizing to me. She wanted to get back to the girls at the sober house. I texted that I would call the police, but Jenna begged me not to." The man had driven them from New Hampshire to Springfield, Massachusetts, and picked up drugs. Now they were heading back to Vermont. Jenna told her mother they had drugs worth fifty thousand dollars in the car. She was a known drug user, and she didn't want to go to jail. "She kept saying, 'I know too much, Mom, and I owe them too much money. They're going to kill me.' What could I do?" Dawn stared at me.

I wondered if she expected me to offer a possibility that she had missed. "There was nothing you could do once she got in that car."

Eventually, the driver stopped at a house in rural Orange, Vermont, population less than a thousand. Still in Costa Rica, Dawn discovered no Uber or taxi service exists in Orange. "Finally, I had to text and tell her, 'I can't find anyone to get you.'" Dawn grimaced. "I mean, what was I going to do? Have my mom go pick her up from a place where people have guns? Or my son? He has a baby. There was no one I could ask. Jenna typed back, 'I think they're going to shoot me.'"

During this, the Tatros boarded a flight from Costa Rica to the tiny Burlington airport. "At midnight, when the plane hit the tarmac in Burlington and we came back into service, my phone started binging like crazy. 'Where are you, Mom? Come get me, Mom!'"

Dawn raced along the empty interstate, panicking. In winter, I knew, stars shine especially brilliantly in the cold. Jenna texted that the men had disappeared into rooms in the house. She was going to run. "Just pick me up wherever I end up." Meanwhile, Greg called the state police. Troopers found Jenna along a road and brought her to the emergency room. Fearing for her life, she had bitten her nails so savagely her hands were covered in blood. "When I showed up at the hospital, she came running to me. 'Mom,' she said, 'I'm okay, I'm okay. I haven't used.' They screened her at the hospital, and she was clean. She was sober, even after all that. We brought her home."

∽

The final days of Jenna's life were chaotic. She pleaded with her parents for permission to pick up clothes from her apartment in a nearby town. When she returned to their house, hours later, she was sober. But the next morning, Greg discovered Jenna on the floor, unconscious from a drug overdose. An ambulance transported her to the local hospital, where she spent the night. Meanwhile, in an unusual ruling, a judge granted Greg custody of his adult daughter, declaring Jenna incapable of making competent decisions, in the hope of aiding the family. When she was discharged after the overdose, the Tatros insisted that Jenna immediately reenroll in treatment. Reluctantly, Jenna agreed to return to the New Hampshire facility, where she was required to again undertake the arduous work of redoing her twelve steps. She begged her parents for time to gather her belongings.

"Big mistake. Terrible mistake," Dawn said quietly. "Jenna put off leaving, puttering around the house, looking for this or that. Finally, around six o'clock in the evening, we all agreed to leave early the next morning. This center was at the other end of New Hampshire, almost in Maine, and it was a lengthy drive to begin that late in the day. We packed the car, and Jenna did the intake over the phone." Dawn picked up one of the photos of Jenna from the coffee table, caressing its cardstock edge with her thumb. "Before we went to bed, we talked for a little while. Jenna was really down. She told us, again, that she had never wanted to be an addict. When we said good night, she said, 'I'll see you in the morning. I love you.'"

I stared at the photo in Dawn's hand, that image of Jenna and her best friend in India, smiling and posing with an elephant. I guessed Jenna had been about twenty, Molly's current age.

"Around eleven that night, Greg checked on Jenna. From upstairs, I heard him shout, 'Call 911!'" For twenty minutes, Dawn and Greg took turns administering CPR. Three times, they tried to revive her with Narcan. When the ambulance arrived, the paramedics asked the couple to step out of the room. "I believed God would save her, because he'd saved her so many times. When the paramedics said they couldn't, I got down on my hands and knees and said, 'My God, you didn't save her. I was so sure you were going to save her!'"

"I'm so sorry . . ."

Despite her tears, Dawn's body tensed in fury. "The sheriff told us the substance Jenna used was pure fentanyl. 'That's homicide,' he told us."

"The drugs were tainted?"

"Intentionally."

"You don't think it was a mistake?"

"No." Staring at me, she let the word lie between us. Then she continued, "After Jenna passed, I was desperate to get some closure. Greg and I tracked down the woman who had sold Jenna the fentanyl. When we showed up at her apartment, she told us that, the day after Jenna died, she called the guy who had given her the drugs and asked if he had heard that Jenna overdosed. He said, 'Oh? Really?' 'That piece of shit,' she said to me."

"Wait. What are you saying?"

"She said he gave her the drugs, knowing they would end up with Jenna. I told law enforcement that we could use this woman to go after him. If she didn't help, she could lose custody of her child. But nothing ever happened. No charges were ever pressed."

"What do you mean? Why not hold him accountable?"

"Law enforcement knew she was more afraid of the gang than she was of any social service agency. She'd never rat him out. The gang would kill her; the state would only take her child."

"You think your daughter was murdered?"

"Yes."

"Honestly . . . I don't know how to respond to that."

She bit the edge of her lower lip. "I know. If I were you, I wouldn't believe me, either. But I'm convinced her death was no accident. Jenna got mixed up with the wrong people. We tried so hard to get her out — so hard. But we failed." Bowing her head, Dawn pressed her palms to her forehead, weeping.

Among the photographs on the table, Dawn had also laid out a handwritten letter from Jenna. From where I sat, I read the lines, which ended, "I just hope you know you are more than a mom to me; you're the best friend a mom could ever be." What the hell happened to this family?

With that sodden Kleenex, Dawn wiped her eyes. "I'm sorry. I miss my daughter so much."

"There's no need to apologize. As a mother, my heart aches for you, but I also admire you and Greg for sharing your story."

"Jenna would have wanted us to speak out. When she first told me about the heroin, I didn't want anyone to know. I just wanted to keep it a secret."

"I know myself why addiction is hidden, and how hiding hinders recovery."

"I didn't see that at the time. When Greg and I realized Jenna was really in deep, we flew to Minnesota and participated in a Hazelden* family program. Jenna didn't come with us, but it was still so powerful for us to sit with other families and their loved ones who were undergoing treatment. When the program ended, everyone was given cups embossed with the word HAZELDEN. One woman refused to take hers; she said she didn't want the Hazelden name in her house. She confessed that she didn't tell anyone when she sent her son away for treatment. But how does she expect her son to recover

---

*The Hazelden Betty Ford Foundation is the nation's largest nonprofit treatment provider for drug and alcohol abuse, with numerous locations.

if she won't even take the cup home? It's unbelievable the amount of families who feel that way. I was once in that camp, too."

"I know," I nodded. "I grew up in a family that kept secrets — who drinks too much, who had a nervous breakdown, who hurt someone else."

"Many families do that, but keeping this particular secret is especially dangerous. When Jenna passed, Greg and I decided that we can't just sit here when so many people are suffering. If we hide what happened, no one can learn from our experience."

"So about your experiences . . . I've heard a lot about your family's plans to open a recovery center. That's why I originally got in touch."

"This was Jenna's vision. She was always asking me to send money for her to share. She knew she was lucky to come from a home that had both love and resources. So many people, by the time they're that far into addiction, have nothing left — no more money, and also no one left in their lives. She kept telling me, 'Mom, when I'm well, we'll team up together, and we'll be unstoppable. We'll help so many people. We're going to educate people about this addiction. We're a great team.' Jenna always wanted to save somebody. That was her dream."

Dawn walked over to the bar and straightened the envelopes in the basket. I couldn't help but wonder if the Tatros did much entertaining any longer. "I want to give you something." She handed me a laminated copy of Jenna's obituary, featuring a smaller version of that photograph in their kitchen. At the very bottom was a small colored drawing of a single sunflower. "This seems heartless, but at one point, I told Jenna she had lost all her friends, that she'd allowed the addiction to take everything from her. I did it to try to goad her to get better. But later I learned that Jenna had a lot of people who loved her and got better because of her. All nineteen women from her sober house came to her wake, and so many people told us Jenna had helped them get clean. One of the girls who spoke at her funeral told me that, when she first met Jenna, she didn't even want to be around her; Jenna was so bubbly, and she had a glow that made it hard to look at her. At the time, this girl was ninety pounds and struggling with a heroin addiction. Jenna was ahead of her in the program and assured the girl she'd meet her in sober living. 'When you detox and start feeling better, we'll have so much fun,' Jenna told her. Weeks later, when the girl arrived at the sober house in a van, Jenna ran out and put her arms around her friend, saying, 'You're here! You're here!' After Jenna's death, her friend told me she had been like, no way, I'm never going to succeed at getting clean."

I slid the hard plastic sheet into my knitting bag. "Is she still sober?"

"Last I spoke with her, yes. It's been maybe eight months."

"You said the wake was in the church you bought?"

"We didn't own it at the time. It was Presidents' Day weekend, and every large space had been booked for months. Even though it had been years since services were held there, our family and friends cleaned it up. Greg and I were married in the church, and Jenna was baptized there."

"And you're going to turn it into a recovery center?"

The edge of her mouth bent up in a glimpse of a smile. "We want it to be a community center for people in recovery. We'll hold meetings, sober events, and fundraisers. Our focus will be on healing. We have so many people already signed up as volunteers. A retired woman who worked in a bank offered to teach budgeting. Others have offered to mentor people in gardening, jewelry making, cooking, yoga, and meditation. Downstairs will be offices for counselors. Upstairs in the community space we'll have talent night and game night and invite in the community. People are going to start saying, 'Hey, people in recovery aren't bad people. These people are us.'"

"Sounds like you've gotten a huge amount of community support."

"It's been tremendous. We've been given so many gifts, and numerous people have offered to help. We've been approached about building a community health center in the parking lot for health and dental care, with a pharmacy and a MAT team. The neighbors on that street didn't welcome this project, though. Greg and I offered to buy the houses by the church and convert them to sober living. We know how hard it was for Jenna to find sober housing. There's an incredible shortage of spaces."

"How was your offer received?"

"We talked to the owners of every house on that street. One woman told me that she'd heard what we were doing, and she wasn't happy about it. 'We don't want those people here,' she said. I told her, 'I want to tell you something. You see that house over there? Unfortunately, I know that gangs arrive there on Thursday and distribute drugs until Sunday. You want them there, instead of people in recovery, who, if they do use, will have to leave? You're happier risking a random bullet or getting stolen from because they need money? That's who's there now. My daughter was not a bad person, and she shouldn't be labeled as one.' The woman looked at me and said, 'I know your daughter wasn't.' I told her that the people we are trying to help aren't, either. She admitted she felt better after we talked. That's what we need to do: educate people and break down that stigma."

"You know," I said, marveling that I was in a stranger's living room, talking about such intimate experiences, "it's been almost a year and a half since I started on this journey. If there's one thing I've learned, it's that overcoming addiction requires incredible courage and endurance — both from the sufferer and those around them."

"Jenna would agree. She believed she could change the world person by person, like with her friend she met in that last rehab." Dawn sat beside me, so close I saw the weave of her dark-purple shirt. "Here's one more thing. The other morning, one of Jenna's high school friends texted me. Jenna had appeared to her in a dream standing in a field of yellow flowers. Not ten minutes later, I received a message from another one of her high school friends. 'You're never going to believe this,' she wrote, 'but Jenna came to me in a dream last night.' It was the same dream. 'Jenna wanted me to tell you she's okay. She's at peace. She's making a difference. She's opening doors that there's no other way could have been opened." She clenched her phone. "I wish you could have met Jenna. I have so many little things I saved from her, like voice messages. In one of them, she was calling to say that the moon was especially beautiful, so big and full, and I should go out and see it. These dreams mean so much to me, because I know she's still with us. I feel her presence, every day."

I wiped my tears with the heel of my hand. "Thank you for sharing this story. I'd love to come back and meet Greg and visit the church, if that's all right."

"Of course." Dawn walked me to the door.

I bent down and strapped on my sandals. When I stood again, we embraced, and then I hurried down the steps.

As I drove down the dirt road, flanked by thick, leafy woods on either side, something needled me, hovering around the edges of my thinking as I thought about our conversation. I followed Route 15, winding along the river, then headed up the narrow pass between Hardwick and Woodbury to drop interlibrary loan books at the library and pick up my paycheck, which the treasurer had left on my desk. As I emerged out of that twisting pass, what had been gnawing around the edges of my thinking leaped out in front of me, as if a white-tailed deer from the trees lining the pass had run into the road. Surely Dawn would have wished for Jenna to have had an ordinary life: finishing college, building a career, getting married, and having children. Instead, her life careened down an unexpected road. But despite her profound addiction, Jenna had quietly helped so many people. I remembered listening to an NPR segment, years ago, featuring a prison inmate who noted that an ax is both a tool and a weapon. So many times I'd assured my daughters that their weaknesses were their strengths, too. In Jenna's story that became save another life, but lose yours.

I turned into the library parking lot and sat for a moment, my hands on the steering wheel. I imagined Jenna running out of the sober house to greet her anxious friend, exclaiming, "You're here! You're here!" In a few weeks, Jenna would be dead.

∽

At the library, I grabbed my paycheck from my desk. When I returned to the parking lot, I saw Krystal, the patron who returned books smelling of cigarettes, standing beside my car. Wearing cotton-candy-pink shorts and a matching tube top, she had a quarter-sized scab on one knee.

"Hey, there," I said.

"You going to town?"

"Yeah. Want a ride?"

"I was gonna ask for one."

We got in the car, and I turned north on Route 14, heading back to Hardwick. While I drove, Krystal stared straight ahead, leaning against the passenger door. "Tom was on a rant. He just gets so mad, and I can't deal with that. He's frustrated at not working, but he had a job, and he blew it."

"Where was he working?"

"He was on a crew building that house up on the Cabot Road. He had a ride and all, too. But then he didn't show, just 'cause he didn't want to. I mean, come on, man; it's paying work. They said don't come back. I'm thinking it's time for me to go back to my gram's, up in Irasburg. She's good to me. She's not like the people who birthed me. That's what I call them. I refuse to call them anything else."

Krystal unrolled the window. The breeze fluttered her bangs. "Every so often, I hitch a ride to Irasburg to visit her. It's forty-five minutes by car, but if you're walking — good luck. That could take you all day."

"I bet."

"My gram's house is real nice. She's got my white dog, Taffy, who's a sweetheart."

"Are you headed there now?"

"Naw, I got stuff to do. You can drop me at the liquor store up ahead."

I pulled in and parked at the pumps. "I guess I might as well fill up while I'm here. Good luck!"

"Yeah. Thanks."

While I pumped gas, I squinted in the sunlight, thinking about Dawn in her plum shirt and sunny kitchen, grieving for her daughter. In the store, I paid for the gas, then asked the clerk to ring up a sleeve of six Klondike bars.

"Eating ice cream is a good idea today," the clerk said. "Might as well. The snow's going to start falling again before we know it."

I took my change and picked up the cold package from the counter. "Not this week, at least."

Outside, I had just opened my car door when Krystal reappeared. "Need a ride farther?" I asked. "I'm headed to the other side of town to get my daughter."

"I was wondering if you maybe got two dollars? I could get Tom a pack of cigarettes. That'd make him happy for the night."

I slid a five-dollar bill from my wallet and handed it to her. "You want an ice cream bar, too?"

"Heck, yes."

I tore the plastic sleeve, pulled out one, and gave it to her. I bent into the car and laid the cold package on my passenger seat. When I looked up, Krystal was walking away from me, unwrapping her ice cream. Without looking back, she disappeared around the squat cement block building.

I drove through town until I reached the carpool turnout. There I got out of my little car and stood at the edge of the field, planted in orderly rows with hemp plants. The air, stagnant on this hot summer morning, was redolent with the ripening hemp's spicy scent and its undertones of skunkiness. Wild cup plants grew along the riverbank, taller than me and lavish with gold blossoms shaped like sunflowers that fit in the palm of my hand. Monarch butterflies flitted among the blossoms, their orange and black wings flickering. Could Jenna really appear in a dream in a field of yellow flowers? Why not? Who was I to define the possibilities of this world?

Jessica's blue Subaru pulled up.

Gabriela stepped out, carrying her backpack, her hair damp and curling at the ends from swimming in Heather's pond.

Through Jessica's unrolled window, I handed her and Lucia Klondike bars. "Awesome," Jessica said. "See you tomorrow morning, same time." She backed her car around and then waved through the open window as she pulled into traffic.

Standing on the roadside beside me, Gabriela peeled the wrapper from an ice cream. "You never get these. I didn't even know you could buy a whole package."

I unwrapped the silver foil from one, too. "Seemed like a perfect day for this. How was camp?"

"Funny. The little kids think everything Lucia and I do or say is super smart. I suggested to Eva that she paint a cactus on her tile. Then she put a tractor under her giant cactus. I thought to myself, *Whaaat? Tilling up sand?*"

Just then, Molly's black Honda rushed into the turnoff. She leaped out of her car, wearing fuchsia scrubs and mirrored sunglasses. "Is my family having a roadside party without me?"

"Klondike?" I offered her the last one.

"Hand it over. How was your visit with the Tatros?"

"Painful. They're an inspiring couple — but what a price. They lost their daughter."

A battered tan Volvo station wagon hurtled by. The driver didn't wave to us, hands clenched on the steering wheel, kicking up a cloud of dust behind him.

"Slow down, buddy," Molly said. "Enjoy the day." She held out her hands. "Do you have anything to clean up with? I don't want to get my steering wheel all yucky."

I shuffled through the library books on the backseat. Beneath the dog-eared Vermont atlas was my gray scarf. Using my water bottle, I dampened the cloth, wiped my sticky fingers, then handed it to Molly.

"Your scarf?"

"Go ahead."

Molly scrubbed her hands.

"Can I use it, too?" Gabriela asked.

"Wait your turn, little sis."

In jest, Gabriela tugged the gray material, and Molly pulled back, ripping the scarf.

"Oof." Gabriela winced.

"Don't sweat it," I said gently, taking back the gray and blue cloth, sugary-sticky and damp, worn from washing and ragged at one end.

"You once wore that everywhere," Molly said. "Like a security blanket."

"Not anymore. Let's go home."

Gabriela said, "I'm riding with Molly." The girls got in Molly's car. Through the open window, I saw Gabriela fiddle with the radio, then my daughters looked at each other and giggled. Then Molly turned onto Route 15 and drove out of my sight.

I stood for a moment longer, holding that soiled cloth in my hand. Then, piece by piece, I ripped the cotton into thin strips and laid the fraying pieces loosely over a branch of a nearby apple tree, wild and unpruned, for a bird in search of material to repair its nest. I tucked one rag in my jean pocket, for a keepsake.

fourteen

Stitching Together the Unstitched

On an overcast autumn afternoon, I returned to Johnson to meet Greg Tatro and learn more about Jenna's House, the nonprofit he and Dawn started in the former church. The stucco building is an anomaly in white clapboard Vermont, elevated slightly from the road on a dead-end street a few minutes from the center of the village. Though its interior was stripped of pews, the bell tower and cross still preside over its pitched roof. A row of mature maple trees flanks its ample front yard, and the backyard is hemmed in by thick woods.

For the first time, I wore the violet sweater I had spent the past year knitting. The previous evening, I cast off the neck and sewed in the loose, dangling ends of yarn. At breakfast, Molly and Gabriela admired the sweater, rubbing their fingers across the gold flowers I had stitched along the hem.

"You're actually going to wear it?" Molly asked. "After all that work?"

"I'm going to wear this sweater until it's shreds. You can bury me in it."

"Wow. What drama," Gabriela said. She stuck her spoon in her bowl of oatmeal.

At the church, I parked in the nearly full lot and walked through the propped-open front doors. The building was under construction, the floor strewn with tools and drop cloths. "I'm looking for Greg Tatro," I mentioned to a woman sitting at a round table near the door where she was sorting through cardboard boxes of used clothing. In our email exchange, Dawn had told me that Jenna's House was organizing a rummage sale that weekend as a fundraiser. The woman pointed across the room to a man writing on a dry-erase board hung on the wall. "That's him."

I made my way around the multiple round tables piled high with board games and tchotchkes. "Greg? I'm Brett Stanciu. I met your wife a month or so ago at your house."

"Sure. I heard about you." With a mustache and square glasses, Greg reached out and shook my hand. "Dawn said you two had a good talk. You're interested in what we're doing here?"

"Very much."

"This board is a good place to get a sense for what we're up to." He pointed to a diagram he was working on. "I keep track of all the finances for Jenna's House here. I want this to be an open process." The expenses, beginning with the church's purchase price, were on one side, and the revenue and gifts — from pro bono attorney work to construction debris removal — were listed on the other side. "We used Jenna's life insurance policy to purchase the church. It kind of sucked that we had to start there," he said in a steady, low voice. The last section of the board showed the first requests for monetary assistance by people recovering from substance abuse. To receive money from the nonprofit, people must submit a budget for how they plan to spend the funds, whether it's for going back to school or attending a training program. "For someone trying to beat a habit, who may not have housing, a job, family, or even friends, a thousand dollars is a lot of money. To us," he said, shrugging, "it's not so much."

Dawn walked in and dropped an armful of folded quilts on a nearby table. Wearing a zipped-up black jacket, she flashed us a warm smile. "Hello again. I see you and Greg met."

"Thanks for asking me back. There's a lot happening here. I mean, your volunteers alone —" I nodded toward the half-dozen women sorting through donations.

"Some are family," she said, "and others are friends or folks who answered our plea for help. Come see the basement kitchen. It's enormous. We haven't even started renovating there yet." She led me down a dimly lit stairway. "We're in the process of talking to the recovery center in Morrisville about using the rest of the basement for more office space for their counselors."

Following behind me, Greg added, "We just want the space to be used. We know the center doesn't have much funding, so we're not asking for rent. If they can put something toward the property taxes, or pay the electricity bill, that would be fine. We're not looking to make a profit. Believe me, that's not the goal."

In the windowless kitchen, we leaned against the wooden cabinets that lined the room, floor to ceiling. Though the counters were completely bare, I easily imagined how the space had hosted countless lunches, baptisms, weddings, and funerals.

"What is your goal?" I asked. The heat hadn't been turned on yet for the fall season, and the room was chilly. I was glad I had worn my sweater.

Greg said, "Part of our mission is to provide services, from health care to counseling. Jenna saw firsthand that so many people with substance abuse issues don't have a family to call on when they need help. If you're sick because every tooth is rotten in your head, it's that much harder to get — and stay — sober. But the wider vision of what we're trying to do is focused on education. Dawn and I didn't know anything about addiction when we started down this path with Jenna. Like so many people, we didn't understand addiction is a disease. She really could not get herself out, much as we were all pulling for her. Now we're trying to share some of what we learned the hard way."

"Beyond health and dental care, counseling, and a MAT program, are there other resources you'll offer? What would have helped Jenna that you couldn't give her?"

"The employment thing." Greg said. He pressed his lips together tightly. "Employment was the place Jenna couldn't get through. If she had, that might have made a huge difference. We want to help people rebuild their sense of purpose by working. Our plan is to partner with businesses in the community, and people can start with small steps, beginning with twenty hours a week or so, and see how that goes."

In the chill, Dawn tugged the sleeves of her jacket over her wrists. "Jenna could sell anything. She worked in a hardware and homeware store our family owned, and she could sell, say, shoes to anyone. 'Hey,' she'd say, 'those look fantastic on you.' Jenna knew and loved cars, so I encouraged her at one point to apply for a job at a nearby dealership. I built her up and gave her all this encouragement. She called me after the interview and said she knew she had nailed it. Of course she did. She was beautiful, just stunning, and sharp as a tack when she was sober. But when she walked out, she overheard someone in the office say, 'Awesome interview, but there's no way we'll hire her. Everyone around town knows she's an addict.' That was it. She told me, 'I'm always going to be an addict. No one's ever going to take a chance on me.'"

Footsteps creaked the upstairs floorboards. A man shouted, "Looks great!"

Crying, Dawn continued, "What if the dealership had taken a chance on her? I've asked myself that question so many times."

"You mean, what if they hadn't just seen her as an addict? What if they had been able to see beyond that stigma?"

"Yes." Dawn dabbed her eyes with a crumpled Kleenex. "What if —?"

The three of us stood in a small space beside the kitchen counter. I grabbed the corner of the center island, weeping, too. I fervently hoped this couple's plans would come to fruition, that this empty kitchen would again be filled with the fragrance of simmering soup, the sink cluttered with dirty dishes and mounds of soap bubbles, and children running in to swipe cookies. "Your plans make so much sense, and if anyone can succeed at this community model, I believe you will. But at what a cost to you two?"

Clearing his throat, Greg said, "Jenna was our daughter, and we loved her. When she passed, we knew we'd lost the battle with her, but we can still help people by making Jenna's vision a reality. It helps with our own grieving, too. I can't wait to see the first person walk in and walk out of here on their own. When they do, I'm going to shake their hand and give them a hug." He studied Dawn. "That'll happen."

Dawn stared at the floor, crying, wiping her eyes with that disintegrating Kleenex.

∽

We returned to the main floor, where Dawn disappeared among the tables mounded with stuffed cardboard boxes. Half listening to Greg as he explained the repairs needed for the exterior stucco, I looked around the space, noting the narrow choir loft built against the back wall.

Greg said, "I've come here on a few days when it's sunny and pulled out a chair on the porch, to think and write stuff down." He tilted his head back and appraised the domed ceiling. "Our little town could use some uplifting. There aren't many places where people can simply get together anymore."

"It's a sweet little place." We paused in the entryway, gazing out at the red and yellow maples, random patches of color against the gray sky. "These days, everyone's so busy working that no one seems to have time or energy to put into groups like the ladies auxiliary that used to keep people connected."

"We've come unstitched," Greg said simply. "We've got to stitch the darn thing back together. I hadn't thought of it that way before, but that's what this project is doing."

A woman in a red blazer deposited two stuffed brown paper bags of clothes on a nearby table and called to Greg, "Good luck!"

He raised his hand. "Thank you!"

We walked around a table of children's books. A water-stained hardback copy of *Heidi* lay on top of a pile, one of my own childhood favorites. On its faded cover, the plucky heroine in a short blue dress who loved toasted cheese sandwiches beamed, surrounded by alpine wildflowers. "One thing that surprised us when we started this project is how many visitors came, including the governor. We also learned about the need for someone in the private sector to take the lead. Slowly, I began to realize that tackling the opioid crisis isn't something that can be legislated. Sure, laws can, and should, be tightened. The gangs who sold Jenna that junk should go to jail. The pharmaceutical companies who manufacture it should pay the consequences, too. But the harder, trickier part? The part where we look at ourselves as a community and take stock?" He shook his head. "You can't legislate that." He laid his hand on *Heidi*, one thumb rubbing its faded spine. "Someone had to stand up and say, publicly, 'Hey, there's not an us or them in addiction.' If we keep thinking that some people are good and others are pariahs, we're never going to solve this problem."

"You mean," I said, "don't see only the addiction. See the person."

"Exactly. That can be really difficult, and maybe it even seems impossible. But I have to believe that we can do it."

With my sweater's cuff, I smeared tears from my cheeks.

"We're just trying to do a little good here." Greg gestured around the space with one hand. "This isn't about Dawn and me. We just happened to be people in a particular place, at a particular time, with some resources. We would never have chosen this."

A man wearing jeans stained with thumbprints of white plaster asked Greg, "Can you come take a look at this?"

"Go on," I said. "Thank you so much for talking to me."

He shook my hand and disappeared through the door.

Before leaving, I stood for a moment in the dusty room's center, surrounded by round tables covered with community donations. Some of these boxes and bags probably held not much at all, bent aluminum pans or long-unwanted coats from attics or basements, but among the piles certainly lay treasures, too — an embroidered child's dress or a man's brand-new suit. Outside as I walked to my car in the parking lot, cars streamed in to unload. In the dreary afternoon, the headlights shone as small luminaries.

I drove away, the surrounding hills scattershot with random patches of brilliant gold and scarlet foliage. In a few more days, those pretty leaves would fall in a single hard storm or simply drop to the ground, the fall finished. For months, skeletal branches and twigs would etch forlornly against the sky.

⤚⤙

I had stayed longer than I intended with the Tatros. Gabriela would be finished with soccer practice soon and looking for the ride home I had promised. Driving along the river, I thought back to that bleak January morning in the library, the day after John Baker died. On the table, I discovered the china cup half filled with Woodbury spring-water. Standing there alone, pondering that teacup, I saw that in the last moments of his life the man had been thirsty.

Without warning, the library door had opened, and the chair of the town's select board walked in. Wordlessly, he embraced me. I pressed my face into the lapels of his black wool peacoat and wept. I knew nothing of him, save his name, Skip Lindsay, and that he had once lived with his first wife in the town where I grew up, Goffstown, New Hampshire. He lived beside Glen Lake, where I had ice skated as a girl when the lake froze solid in the heart of winter.

When he left, I was alone again. I held up that teacup to the scant winter daylight streaming through the window, swirling around those few swallows of remaining water, wondering what I would do next.

⤚⤙

When John Baker died, I began the harrowing work of examining myself — how I have grown since getting sober, but also where I have failed. Since I was a child, writing has been the way I've under-stood the world, first through reading fiction and writing a novel about living in rural Vermont, then through nonfiction as a journal-ist, essayist, and blogger about single motherhood. As I started asking questions of myself and people around me, I naturally turned to writing to make sense of what I was learning. I began to wake before dawn and write before going to work, spurred to understand my role in John Baker's suicide. In my nighttime drive with Gabriela, I told her how, as a young woman, I conquered my fear of the dark so I could live in rural Vermont. Likewise, two decades later, I knew on an intuitive level that I had to banish my fear of addiction so I could move on with my life.

As I reached out to community members and read extensively, I realized that addiction is propelled not only by the hand that lifts the drink or fills a syringe but also by a plethora of powerful factors, including genetic composition and trauma. While addiction had always appeared to me primarily as the sad story of individual sufferers, for the first time, I began to see how addiction spreads like cancer through our society. Addiction is big business, fueled by a criminal network — from small-time dealers like Sam McDowell to the gang that ensnared Jenna Tatro — and wealthy corporations that profit from pushing powerfully addictive pharmaceuticals. As Chief Cochran noted, when one supply, like black-market Big Boys, is cut off, another, such as heroin, gushes in. Who can possibly overpower vast criminal networks, often better funded than small-town police departments? Who can successfully stand up to the Sackler family or to pharmaceutical companies with their bottomless resources? Beyond that, no one in Vermont, let alone the nation, has a comprehensive plan for how to dampen the demand for these substances. Generational poverty, systemic racism, a widening disparity in wealth, and fragmented communities factor into this complex equation.

In the face of this seemingly hopeless situation, I doubted myself. Why keep asking questions? What good would it do for me to understand something I was powerless to change? So as I scrutinized the colossal forces of history and greed, I hoped merely to unearth a few success stories, a modest silver lining in the storm clouds of despair. Much to my surprise, though, I began to recognize that individual lives are what matters. In truth, the Sackler family members occupy one extreme of human behavior; as I asked, I met person after person — seemingly ordinary people — who unhesitatingly offered me aid and insight, speaking with me for one primary reason: to help others. Some of these people are portrayed in these pages. Many others never appeared.

Early on, I was introduced to Shauna Shepard, who risked her own recovery to tell her story. In a world where the loudest and most flamboyant words are often acclaimed, solitary acts of quiet courage are often unnoticed. Yet those small acts shape and change our lives.

"I want to help," she told me, "just one person."

I am that person.

Shauna gave me — reluctant, frightened me — the courage to scrutinize my own addiction. As I did, my determination to hide my own addiction and my shameful struggles began to wither, like a skin I had outgrown.

As I wrote this book, I returned to Raymond Carver's short story about drinking and recovery, "Where I'm Calling From," which alludes to Jack London's story "To Build a Fire" — the classic high school read featuring a man lost in the wilderness. After several attempts, the man finally ignites a small fire, "but then," Carver writes, "something happens to it . . . Night is coming on." The desolation of night emerges all through these pages, from how Sam McDowell's life dwindled to the next fix to Meg Goulet saying, "I did go down." All through my life, I've struggled with night coming on, once upon a time using the warmth of alcohol to stave off that fear, and now fortressing myself with writing, books, and knitting. Recovery, I finally began to glimpse, is no magical kingdom or peaceful place of respite but instead living day by day in this flawed and mortal world.

This book makes no claim to offer any formula for a way out. It's impossible not to acknowledge the bitter despair of addiction and the merciless reality that some sufferers never elude its bonds; that the requisite pound of flesh so often paid for escape becomes an entire body of flesh; that, for every person like Meg, who emerged from the darkness of addiction to help others, an early grave claims another. In the battle against addiction, there are clear advantages, including affluence, race, and education. But the murkiness of luck, or perhaps the fickleness of fate, has its role, too.

Most unexpectedly while writing this book, I witnessed how love binds people more fiercely than even the shackles of addiction. I saw this driving force in my love for my daughters and theirs for me; in Shauna and Sam and Meg's families, too; and, heartbreakingly, in the Tatro family. The love I witnessed was never golden and pure; the people I wrote about, like myself, have done unforgivable acts to those they love most dearly. And yet, as long as we're alive, the possibility of redemption shimmers before us, tarnished as our lives might be.

All my life, I've resisted and vilified the attempt to pretty up the world and make light of tragedy, to offer a Band-Aid of Love Cures All to the reality that life is saturated with suffering. Years into sobriety, I have finally realized that none of us can pass through this life without loss and grief, that we all possess what poet Mary Oliver described as our boxes of darkness. How utterly fitting it was that the Tatros chose an empty church to house their place of healing. That church kitchen where I wept with those two grieving parents had collectively celebrated the joy of babies and marriages and anniversaries, but it had also sustained its parishioners through funerals and tragedies.

As I finish writing this book, I wish I could testify that today I joyfully greet strangers. I don't. I'm cautious and careful. I worry acutely about my own daughters and where their lives may lead. I'm perhaps more wary than ever of addiction's might, of the darkness that can and does swallow lives whole. If asked, I may not step up to the high mark Shauna set. But what has changed is this: When I encounter behavior that puzzles or troubles me, I've learned to pause and inquire, *Why? What's the larger story here?* Ask enough and you'll find a concealed chain of circumstances, a broken body, or an anguished heart.

∽

For years, I believed that I had caused my addiction, and so, by extension, I took sole responsibility for my recovery. But the starker and less self-indulgent truth is that neither my addiction nor my healing were entirely my doing. Along my journey, I have been given countless undeserved gifts — a book to guide me, the thousandth opportunity to get clean, and much more. When I struggled mightily to free my daughters and myself from a domestic life on the edge of violence, a woman I never met at the tax department made it possible for me to sell the house and move; a judge counseled me to "be careful, ma'am," where the law held no teeth; and a mechanic underbilled me for years. For every neighbor who hired my ex-husband and paid him under the table, a friend would stop by with a loaf of bread or a dozen eggs from their chickens.

And although I couldn't see it at the time, when I was at the very bottom of addiction's well, I was flung the lifesaving rope of my daughters' love, and I grasped it. This book is the cord I've unfurled into the abyss. If even one person catches these words, know this: Your life is worth saving.

∽

Back in Hardwick on that autumn afternoon, I parked at the high school and got out of my car. The sun was descending toward the round hump of Buffalo Mountain. A single heron winged across the sky. Still wearing my sweater, I walked toward the soccer fields. In blue soccer shorts and T-shirts, my daughter and her friend ran to me, their arms outstretched. Giggling, the girls wrapped their arms around me, their crimson cheeks cold against mine, still warm from the car. They were deliriously happy about being offered a wood-stacking odd job earlier that day.

These two girls met when they were eight years old and were awed to discover their first names each had eight letters, and they were exactly the same height. That fall, I took the girls apple picking in a hillside orchard, where they lifted each other up to pick fruit from higher branches. Sunlight spilled through the leaves and onto the unmown grass. The autumn air was sweet with the scent of fallen apples, bruised and slightly mashed, already beginning to turn back into the earth and rot.

The girls ran into the high school to change their clothes, swap cleats for Vans, and gather their backpacks. A mother I knew by sight but not by name got out of a white pickup pocked with rust and joined me on the sidewalk. Although our daughters were in the same grade, we had rarely spoken. She was so much younger than me that I always assumed she had been a teenager when she became a mother. "Kids finished yet?" she asked.

"They went in to change."

"I love your sweater. Did you knit it?"

"Sure did. Took me a long time. All that ripping apart and reknitting." I stretched out my arms, showing off the fancy gold flower pattern over the lavender cuffs, two inches of painstaking work. On my right wrist, a strand of gold yarn had snagged loose, by a nail at the church construction site or maybe a thorny bush.

"Oooh." She touched the unraveling yarn. "I'm a handworker, too. I have a crochet hook in my pickup. Let me fix this for you. Okay?"

I nodded. As she walked away, I noticed a tattoo of a red dragon on the left side of her neck beneath her blond crew cut, its wings and long tail wrapping around her pale skin.

When she returned, she gently lifted my forearm in her hands and fingered the loose yarn, its crisp color not yet sullied by wear. Deftly, she wound her silver crochet hook into the gold petal. As her shoulder rose and fell, the dragon's tail flickered in and out beneath the collar of her sweatshirt.

Gym bag slung over her shoulder, Gabriela emerged from the school. "What's up?"

"Loose thread."

The woman removed her crochet hook and let go of my arm. "All set, for now. Look me up when you want another miracle performed with yarn. I'm not so hot with the loaves and the fishes, but give me yarn and — whoa, baby — I'll knock it out of the park."

Standing between her and Gabriela, I rotated my wrist, the gold yarn iridescent in the gloaming. "It's perfect," I pronounced. Suddenly silly, I bowed to her.

"Well, perfect for a heartbeat's worth of time, at least." She stuck that thin silver hook over her ear, then sauntered across the lot, hands in her overall pockets, to where her daughter waited in their pickup. In the driver's seat, she cranked over the engine, then unrolled the window as she pulled across the lot. She stuck out her arm and waved. "So long!"

Her daughter called out from the passenger seat, "See you tomorrow, Gabby!"

We waved back, then got into my Toyota. "I had the best geometry class today," Gabriela said. "So, Mr. Heller . . ." she began. Listening, I drove us through the village, across the river, and up the hill to our home.

In the kitchen, Gabriela mixed butter and flour and a splash of maple syrup in a bowl for biscuits. With frost in the forecast, I knelt before the woodstove and scraped the embers together in a heap. Flames flickered around the dry birch bark. Tenderly, I breathed on the coals and kindled a fire against the night.

acknowledgments

Support to complete the writing of this book was generously provided by the Vermont Arts Council and the Vermont Arts Endowment Fund at the Vermont Community Foundation. I am also grateful for the support of the Woodbury Community Library trustees, particularly Sara VanHof.

I am immensely indebted to Shauna Shepard, Meg Goulet, Sam McDowell, Josh Bull, and Dawn and Greg Tatro, who shared their stories and answered my questions. Readers who want to learn more about the Tatros' mission to prevent substance abuse and offer support through recovery will find information at *jennaspromise.org*.

Jeri Wohlberg, Katie Whitaker, Michelle Salvador, Bryanne Castle, Aaron Cochran, Dave Yacovone, and Christina Nolan patiently gave me a view into their worlds. Their invaluable insights regarding the complexity of addiction helped me understand the wider and often unseen connections that link all of us.

I am grateful to Chip Fleischer and Steerforth Press. Rebecca Radding's keen editorial skills rendered *Unstitched* a far better book. A thousand thanks, Rebecca.

Nikolai Stanciu and Jess Durocher fed my daughters and provided me with bursts of writing time.

Last, but never least, my daughters, Molly and Gabriela, bore the writing of this book with grace and good humor. You two are the light of my life.

readers' group guide

questions for discussion

1. *Unstitched* opens when a man breaks into a one-room rural Vermont library. Readers accompany Stanciu on her journey as she reaches out to strangers, who range from medical workers and law enforcement officers to people in recovery. Discuss which characters are especially resonant, and why.

2. The author asks hard questions about opioid misuse. What insight does she gain about who becomes addicted?

3. As Stanciu explores the complexities of substance misuse through hearing personal stories, the author confronts how she's stigmatized others, despite her own struggles with addiction. Has *Unstitched* made you look at others in your community in different ways, or caused you to reflect on your own particular views?

4. *Unstitched* acknowledges that fear often accompanies addiction. Stanciu's house is robbed; much worse, she meets two parents who insist their daughter was murdered by gang members when she pursued recovery. How does Stanciu battle her own fear? In what ways does Stanciu believe that fear of crime contributes to the power of addiction?

5. How does Stanciu envision lessening the stigma against people who misuse substances would aid in healing in individuals and communities?

6. As her quest unfolds, Stanciu witnesses that individual actions have profound consequences. "I want to help," Shauna Shepard insisted, "just one person." What are other examples of individual action, for good or ill, in the book?

7. *Unstitched* acknowledges that there are no easy answers to substance misuse. Addiction is braided into the multi-faceted complexities of society — the disparity of privilege and wealth, the vulnerableness of childhood, a frayed spiritual and communal life. Discuss how Stanciu emphasizes these factors.

8. How does the metaphor of darkness and light unfold in the book?

9. Stanciu writes, "In the battle against addiction, there are clear advantages, including affluence, race, and education. But the murkiness of luck, or perhaps the fickleness of fate, has its role, too." Discuss how privilege and circumstances work out for different people in *Unstitched*.

10. The book culminates when Stanciu meets a couple — Greg and Dawn Tatro — who lost their daughter to an overdose. Can you share an experience of your own, or example of someone in your community, when individual choice made a positive difference? Do individuals and communities have a meaningful role in healing addiction?